T0318322

Psychosocial Support for Humanitarian Aid Workers

Humanitarian aid workers are trying to make a difference in an increasingly dangerous world. *Psychosocial Support for Humanitarian Aid Workers: A Roadmap of Trauma and Critical Incident Care* highlights the risks of such work, educates professionals responsible for their duty of care, and brings together current thinking to promote collaborative working to support the carers of our world.

From the humanitarian aid worker trying to organise support amongst chaos, to the professional offering a safe place for recovery, all of these individuals are at risk of becoming traumatised. Therefore, it is vital that we recognise the psychological risks on these individuals, and that they recognise how they can support themselves, so they can continue to function in the work that they do. This book can be used as a trauma awareness guide for all staff whose work exposes them – directly or indirectly – to trauma, and therefore becomes a risk to their physical or mental wellbeing.

Psychosocial Support for Humanitarian Aid Workers will appeal to all those working in the field of humanitarian aid, counsellors and psychotherapists, emergency first responders, as well as those who are looking to support themselves after surviving trauma.

Fiona Dunkley is a senior accredited MBACP Psychotherapist, Trauma Specialist, Supervisor and Trainer. She is a member of EMDR, UKRCP and ESTSS. Fiona founded FD Consultants, offering psychosocial support and trauma specialist services for humanitarian aid organisations. She has presented on 'Good Morning Britain' as a trauma expert, has published several articles and has been asked to speak at various international conferences.

'Raising standards in psychosocial support for those working on humanitarian response to crises and disaster is only just being recognised by those organisations working in the field. This book is an essential and timely contribution to understanding the need for such support as well as providing a practical guide to establishing systems and approaches. I would urge all those responsible for humanitarian aid workers and indeed, for those responsible for staff or volunteers working in development organisations, to read this book as a matter of urgency and to take on board its recommendations.'

Philip Goodwin, Chief Executive, VSO International

'As the lead in an organisation that works directly with the humanitarian aid sector and sees first-hand the needs of these organisations, this book is a must read.

Psychosocial Support for Humanitarian Aid Workers demonstrates that there is no doubt that self-care and resilience form an essential part of being prepared to undertake the very important work the humanitarian sector do in caring for others. At the other end, Fiona's detailed analysis on the impact of trauma both on an individual and at an organisational level shows it must be treated as the highest of priorities.'

Andrew Lewis, Nomad & TMB CEO

Psychosocial Support for Humanitarian Aid Workers

A Roadmap of Trauma and Critical Incident Care

Fiona Dunkley

Routledge
Taylor & Francis Group

LONDON AND NEW YORK

First published 2018 by Routledge

2 Park Square, Milton Park, Abingdon, Oxfordshire OX14 4RN
52 Vanderbilt Avenue, New York, NY 10017

Routledge is an imprint of the Taylor & Francis Group, an informa business

First issued in paperback 2019

British Library Cataloguing-in-Publication Data
A catalogue record for this book is available from the British
Library

Library of Congress Cataloging-in-Publication Data
Names: Dunkley, Fiona, author.
Title: Psychosocial support for humanitarian aid workers : a
roadmap of trauma and critical incident care / Fiona Dunkley.
Description: Abingdon, Oxon ; New York, NY : Routledge, 2018. |
Includes bibliographical references.Identifiers: LCCN 2017058514|
ISBN 9781138707344 (hardback) | ISBN 9781351782050 (web) |
ISBN 9781351782043 (epub) | ISBN 9781351782036
(mobipocket)
Subjects: LCSH: Humanitarian assistance–Psychological aspects. |
Psychic trauma–Prevention. | Charities–Employees. | Nonprofit
organizations–Employees.
Classification: LCC HV553 .D86 2018 | DDC 363.34/80683–dc23
LC record available at https://lccn.loc.gov/2017058514

ISBN: 978-1-138-70734-4 (hbk)
ISBN: 978-0-367-37189-0 (pbk)

Typeset in Times New Roman
by Wearset Ltd, Boldon, Tyne and Wear

I am dedicating this book to a friend of mine who died giving her life to humanitarian aid work. She wasn't supported to 'listen' to her body when it was screaming at her to stop working, she couldn't 'internalise' the voices of reason recommending that she needed to take time out. Her vision to change the world blinded her to her own self-care. And yet, her passion and work continues to make a difference and her legacy remains to help others. May she rest in peace.

Contents

8 Conclusion: the complete trauma grab bag 111

Acknowledgements

At the heart of this book are aid workers' stories of overcoming critical incidents. A special thank you for their honesty and courage, and providing guidance and inspiration to those who read this book. My focus is to make sure their voices are heard. A thank you to all the aid workers who helped shape this book, from the individuals who offered case studies to those who completed the questionnaire and gave their time for interviews: particularly Christoph Hensch (ICRC), Jon Barden (a contractor working for DFID), Megan Nobert (founder of Report the Abuse), Peter Moore (IT consultant), Steve Ryan (security consultant) and Tristan Clements (regional risk manager).

I want to thank my husband, Darcy Weafer-Cook, for his patience, encouragement and support throughout the last couple of years; his acceptance of my paperwork taking over our house for long periods of time, and putting up with my physical and mental absenteeism whilst I was writing late into the night and throughout weekends.

Cat Carter (Save the Children), shared her story with me over a hot chocolate, and her moving TED talk on 'The impact of disaster' encouraged me to write. Also a thank you to Rolf Carriere (economist and former UNICEF employee) for his inspiring TED talk, 'Healing trauma, healing humanity'.

I owe many thanks to those who took the time to read and critique my drafts: my wonderful niece, Yasmin Dunkley, a fellow kindred spirit wanting to make a difference in the world, striving forward in promoting HIV awareness as a HIV Prevention and Testing Lead at Positive East; my sister, Judy Dunkley, who teaches adolescents the skills of science. My friends and colleagues: Lynn Barnes (psychotherapist), Katie Tong (humanitarian consultant) and Ruth Allan (humanitarian consultant).

A heartfelt thank you goes to my former colleague at Transport for London (TfL) and friend, Beth Glanville. She shares my passion for trauma and caring for the carers. Beth is a psychotherapist working within the Counselling and Trauma Service at TfL, and in private practice. She has generously dedicated her time and commitment to proofreading and editing my drafts. She is a fellow writer and is a sectional editor with the online journal *Contemporary Psychotherapy*. She has written for a number of further publications and has self-published several books under the name of Elizabeth.

Thank you to so many inspiring, motivating and passionate individuals working in the humanitarian sector and all of the wonderful encouragement presented to me whilst writing this book. 'If you want to improve the world, start by making people feel safer' (Porges, 2001). The work aid workers are invested in is clearly part of the solution to making a safer world.

Preface

Psychosocial Support for Humanitarian Aid Workers is a book that aims to psychologically prepare, strengthen and build resilience of aid workers by encouraging good psychosocial care practices for staff exposed to the humanitarian aid sector. Although the focus is on aid workers, this book will help anyone whose work involves direct or indirect contact with traumatic material, those living with or close to someone with post-traumatic stress disorder (PTSD), any individual who is suffering or has recovered from trauma, or anyone who has a general interest in trauma work. All the techniques referred to in this book are useful in supporting and managing symptoms of acute stress and trauma. As Bessel Van Der Kolk, a world-renowned trauma specialist psychotherapist states, 'Trauma is now our most urgent public health issue' (Van Der Kolk, 2014, p. 356). This book aims to enable individuals to recognise the symptoms of trauma, identify when a fellow colleague or loved one may be suffering, and create a resilience toolkit of coping strategies. It offers an educational journey to encourage organisations to review their duty of care policies, critical incident plans, and implement a 'trauma management programme' in supporting their staff, and for humanitarian donors to consider the funding allocations for staff welfare. The material can also be useful for psychotherapists or mental health practitioners who are interested in trauma, and working with emergency first responders or those in the humanitarian sector.

The introduction explores 'the roadmap' to trauma and critical incident care, highlighting the psychological risks to aid workers and exploring the changing face of the humanitarian sector. This is followed by a chapter on 'the mechanics' of trauma, exploring the physiology and neuroscience of trauma, including a clear explanation of how the body and mind are impacted by trauma exposure. Chapter 3 details two aid workers' case studies, the first using Eye Movement Desensitisation Reprocessing (EMDR), and the second using Trauma-Focused Cognitive Behavioural Therapy (TF-CBT). This chapter gives a detailed insight into the therapy work of treating PTSD, which I refer to as the 'support vehicles for recovery'. Chapter 4 offers many resources and techniques for managing acute stress and trauma, with which I encourage the reader to develop their own resilience 'first aid kit' of coping strategies. Chapter 5 examines the psychological management of critical incidents; what I refer to as 'the emergency route'. This chapter focuses on informing organisations how to develop a trauma management programme for staff, which should define support for every stage of a critical incident, from early intervention, trauma-specific treatments and follow-up, right through to recovery. In addition, it encourages humanitarian donors to acknowledge the indirect costs that front-line agencies incur by providing responsible staff psychosocial support services. The sixth chapter takes the reader on a journey through the complete package of care, from pre-, to during and post-deployment psychosocial support. I have referred to this journey as 'the road most travelled', as it is a process that needs to be embedded into the organisational culture. Chapter 8 explores the many facets of the cultural relevance of psychosocial services; the need to have knowledge of the 'local roadmaps', including access to culturally sensitive support and the development of local mental health services, and the consequent challenge of using western norms and staff, as well as the disparity of care between national and international staff. Finally, a list of references to sources of support is offered.

My aim is to balance theory, research and personal stories. This book is the voice of the aid workers, interweaved with personal case studies. As I gathered completed questionnaires and case studies, and as I interviewed aid workers, mental health workers and emergency first responders, I was repeatedly encouraged that this book is necessary. I have been overwhelmed with the level of support and encouragement from the humanitarian sector. In writing this, I hope to have done justice to the cause of highlighting the importance of caring for the carer, as this has been my passion and purpose. Carers deserve to be cared for, as they are the advocates for hope and healing in our world.

Terminology

Psychosocial support: 'Any type of local or outside support that aims to protect or promote psychological wellbeing and/or prevent mental disorder' (IASC, 2017, p. 4). I have used this term throughout the book to refer to any psychological support services.

Staff: full-time, part-time, contractors, volunteers, national, international, local, intern and office- or field-based. The term 'staff' does not take into account the different contractual terms and conditions which apply and vary between, for example, a contractor and a volunteer.

Aid worker: humanitarian workers, those working in development in humanitarian environments, emergency first responders, human rights workers, staff of development organisations, and rescue and relief workers.

Humanitarian organisations: general term to cover all humanitarian organisations, including: community-based organisations, donor governments working in and on emergency settings, International Committee of the Red Cross and Red Crescent (ICRC), International Federation of the Red Cross and Red Crescent (IFRC), international non-government organisations (INGOs), national non-government organisations (NNGOs), national government authorities and United Nations agencies.

Confidentiality/case studies: I have consent to use all the quotes and case studies included herein. If individuals wish to remain anonymous, I have disguised all identifying information and added a pseudonym after each reference (name, country). For material where individuals have given consent to be named, I have added their full name and job title. To protect privacy and confidentiality, all identifying client information has been altered or client consent has been obtained in line with BACP's *Ethical Framework for the Counselling Professions* (BACP, 2016).

Self-care: as with any trauma material the information in this book may be triggering. Please do bear this in mind when reading this book and take a break if necessary. Chapter 4 offers many techniques that can help you if you do begin to feel triggered in any way.

The material in this book has been taken from my own personal and professional experiences by sharing my journey of working in the field of trauma, through supporting emergency first responders – the police, fire fighters, veterans, ambulance personnel and humanitarian aid workers – and supporting clients through issues such as terrorist attacks, kidnapping and hostage-taking, civil unrest and war, assault, sexual violent crime, transport accidents, human trafficking, adoption, traumatic bereavement, childhood abuse and domestic violence.

1 Introduction

The roadmap of psychological risk

As a journalist turned aid worker I thought I was used to dealing with difficult and sometimes traumatising news stories. I've spent years sitting in newsrooms sifting through uncut footage from bomb blasts in Iraq, Afghanistan or Syria. As an editor it was also my job to watch the uncut versions of hostage videos sent from Islamic State or Al Qaeda and decide where that footage should be edited, or indeed if it was too gruesome to go to air at all. I'd also spent time in the field before, travelling to Liberia during the Ebola outbreak and also east Africa to cover stories on poverty, child marriage and malnutrition. I thought I was battle-hardened and could deal with almost anything, so when I was given the opportunity to travel to Sierra Leone following the Ebola outbreak I was keen to go. When I returned I would find myself bursting into tears or be overcome with anger at the slightest thing. I felt constantly on edge, had difficulty sleeping and had awful vivid memories of specific events that would haunt me. It wasn't until several months after I returned home that I admitted to myself I needed help.

(Bianca, UK)

Aid work: the curse of the strong

Working within the field of trauma is deeply moving. I have been doing so for over 17 years, and in my view it is completely unacceptable to continue to hear stories of individuals who have fallen through the net of trauma care. The neuroscience and research of trauma has developed at a great pace over the last two decades. Stories of individuals suffering with trauma symptoms for years make headlines in the western world; and in developing countries research highlights significant numbers of people impacted by trauma as the prevalence of war and natural disasters continue to rise. How can we inform individuals of the impact of trauma, to enable them to be better prepared and able to recognise the signs and symptoms of trauma, and to develop skills to strengthen themselves while supporting their colleagues, family or friends if they are suffering? And if experiencing trauma to some degree is unavoidable, how can we make recovery a right for everyone? My hope is that this book will go some way to offering that. Trauma can lock us into a prison within ourselves, sometimes referred to as 'the enemy within'. This book aims to break the silence of trauma, help to normalise trauma, and provide the reader with the confidence to be trauma-informed. It demonstrates trauma specialist treatments with detailed case studies and provides practical coping strategies and resources for those that are suffering from trauma and acute stress. I also hope this book offers comfort, on the darkest days, for anyone suffering from trauma. It is a book that will support anyone who has experienced trauma, anxiety, stress, burnout, compassion fatigue or vicarious trauma, as it gives an in-depth insight into the world of mental health through the lens of trauma.

As I was speaking to a group of security managers at a humanitarian forum, I became aware that trauma awareness training seemed to be a luxury, due to 'lack of resources'. This book can be used as a trauma awareness guide for all staff whose work exposes them – directly or indirectly – to trauma, and therefore becomes a risk to their physical or mental wellbeing. I suffered from Post-Traumatic Stress Disorder (PTSD) over 20 years ago. At that time, there was very little understanding of the impact of trauma and there was no trauma specialist therapy available to me, but not understanding my symptoms was the most disturbing ailment. I often experience clients feeling the same way:

> not knowing anything about trauma symptoms or PTSD, I thought I was having a nervous breakdown and this was a major mental health collapse. I couldn't see how this would get better, that this was something that could be recovered from, I just thought, this is finally it; I'm losing it for good.
>
> (Omar, Jordan)

Most people recover from trauma naturally, although they can still experience frightening symptoms for several weeks, and therefore to gain an understanding that these symptoms are OK and normal can make such a difference in those early stages. I want this book to offer that knowledge and reassurance, and I strongly believe everyone, with the right specialist help, can recover from trauma.

Aid workers are mostly driven by the belief that the humanitarian imperative comes first and the right to receive humanitarian assistance is a fundamental humanitarian principle, which should be enjoyed by all citizens of all countries. The prime motivation of responses to disaster is to alleviate human suffering amongst those least able to withstand the stress caused by disaster. When humanitarians give aid it is not a partisan or political act but as humanitarian responses have become more prolific and protracted, and humanitarian and development agendas have become more closely linked, aid workers have also started to advocate for equality, justice and empowerment. It is considered that this type of work becomes more than a job:

> This job is not a job. It is so much more than that. It is my life. This job requests every part of me. The aid worker in me has to be strong. This side of me has to manage and make important decisions, which could lead to the life or death of my team members.
>
> (Eileen, Cameroon)

Humanitarian work is inherently stressful, with long working hours, away from family and friends, frequent transitions, security constraints, managing emergencies and making life-saving decisions. Other stressors include: working in warzones and areas of natural disasters, being exposed to suffering and death, witnessing the inhumane treatment of those who are disadvantaged or disempowered, and observing the best and the worst of humanity. Humanitarian aid aims to provide food, clean water, shelter, sanitation, agricultural and livelihood support, education and medical care. Aid workers advocate for justice, speak out against sexual violence and gender inequality, alleviate suffering, manage emergencies, build schools and reduce poverty. Steve Ryan, a security consultant, describes the reasons he experienced cumulative stress:

> years of travelling, often at short notice, to dangerous places; the unforgettable smell of a mass grave in a Lebanese summer; constantly juggling social and work life; hearing the crack of a bullet overhead in Yemen; talking about risk across grand tables in HQ, or plastic picnic tables in the field; a close call in Syria, and guilt-inducing missed calls on my ever-present work phone had all taken its toll.

The case studies shared in this book include individuals who have been attacked, shot at, kidnapped and survived sexual violence. Additionally, and just as importantly, they include stories of individuals who have suffered the effects of cumulative stress and trauma. Trauma can just as easily be the result of cumulative stress, for example from harassment and poor management from organisations: 'I cannot say how much the shock of the explosion had on my stress, but the main stressor which caused what was later diagnosed as PTSD from gradual build-up of stress, was caused by constant harassment from my boss' (William, Australia). All of these experiences were compounded by the lack of support individuals received from their organisations at the time. Self-care, resilience and mindfulness are some of the buzzwords referring to wellbeing and well mental health. This book aims to strengthen our own self-care and resilience, and that of the organisation. A resilient organisation encourages resilient staff, and vice versa.

Aid workers have often said to me that they feel guilty asking for support and instead reach out to unhealthy coping mechanisms to drown out the uncomfortable feelings, such as alcohol, caffeine, nicotine or recreational drugs. They can often overlook their own self-care, in the name of the greater cause. 'I felt guilty if I informed anyone I was suffering. How could I complain, when I was faced with such despair in my work, and others were suffering from so much more?' (John, Norway). Ben Porter, the founder of the Recreation Project, Uganda, and a staff care and psychosocial consultant, refers to a break-down truck to highlight the importance of self-care:

> Whilst jogging down a red-dirt road in the Ugandan countryside, I came across a stranded tow-truck (a breakdown as they call them). My friend looked at me and laughed. What happens when the breakdown breaks down? Double trouble, I replied. The situation just got much worse.

Ben notes that 'staff who are employed to assist those in need can end up breaking down and requiring assistance'. If we don't take care of ourselves first and foremost, we will not be strong or resilient enough to care for others.

I repeatedly hear from aid workers that stigma is one of the main reasons why individuals do not reach out for support. Individuals suffering mental health issues often worry that they will be perceived as 'weak' and, in fact, psychiatrist Tim Cantopher, who wrote the book *Depressive Illness: The Curse of the Strong* (Cantopher, 2012), describes individuals suffering from cumulative stress as resilient and strong. It is the very fact that they are conscientious, dedicated and hard-working that puts them at risk of becoming ill. The aid workers who shared their stories with me were not weak; I met strong, passionate, inspiring and resilient individuals. They also represent the 'change makers' who, at times, are willing to be the lone courageous voice advocating for colleagues who are also struggling, sometimes confronted with a wall of denial and a risk of being scapegoated. These individuals should be embraced as an asset to any organisation and not shamed into resignation, as has happened to some of the individuals whose stories are in this book.

Organisational duty of care

Organisations have made big strides in implementing and improving staff care policies over the last decade, but there is still a great deal to be done to prevent harm to staff faced with working in diverse and risk-fuelled environments, particularly national and local staff. Organisations have an ethical, moral and legal obligation to physically and psychologically take care of their staff, including employees, contractors and volunteers: 'the provision of support to mitigate the possible psychosocial consequences within crisis situations is a moral obligation and a responsibility of organisations exposing staff to extremes' (IASC, 2007, p. 21). A well-implemented organisational response to critical incidents, including an ongoing programme of psychosocial support, is essential. Peer support programmes help to build an internal culture of care and healing based on the humanitarian principles of humanity, neutrality, impartiality and independence (International Red Cross and Red Crescent Movement, 1965).

At the time of writing this book, InterHealth Worldwide, a holistic support service that supported over 500 NGOs, mission and government organisations, and 20,000 individuals, ceased operating. Report the Abuse, a charity formed to support aid workers that had experienced sexual violence, ceased operating. One of the main factors in both instances was lack of funding. I was involved in supporting fire fighters after the Grenfell Tower fire on 14 June 2017, in London, UK, in which 71 people died. The London Fire Service had drastically cut its in-house counselling team, and was desperately requesting *pro bono* therapists. I watched in horror as many therapists, who were not trauma specialists, volunteered and carried out assessments un-vetted. Research showed that the number of fire fighters on long-term mental health leave has increased by 30 per cent over the last six years (Greenwood & Harmes, 2017). These experiences demonstrate that although trauma is talked about more, there is still a significant underfunding and undervaluing of psychosocial services.

In writing this book, I developed a questionnaire to gather data and get a clearer picture of what psychosocial support was available to aid workers from their organisations. I received 30 completed questionnaires covering 18 organisations. Additionally, I gathered 12 detailed case studies, conducted 40 interviews and spoke to hundreds of aid workers over the last two years. I asked aid workers to recommend what psychosocial support they felt would be necessary and beneficial to both support them in their work, and to support them to maintain a healthy lifestyle.

The data collected highlighted that only 20 per cent of aid workers interviewed felt that their organisation offered sufficient psychosocial support. Ninety per cent felt pre-assignment consultations would be helpful and every single individual requested post-assignment consultations, which unfortunately were not routinely offered, even to individuals deployed to high-risk environments. Additionally, many felt unprepared before deployment, and underlined that this was due to a lack of training. Stigma was named as a problem for 85 per cent of aid workers who completed the questionnaire, whether it was stigma of being seen as 'weak' or 'losing out on career development'. Many requested the need for a change in culture, to enable staff to access psychosocial services through the workplace without feeling that they will be negatively judged. This book informs organisations of best-practice psychosocial support for staff. It helps to normalise symptoms of trauma; identify trauma as a workplace risk factor; challenge organisational culture and stigma; and create a holistic and community based approach to recovery.

If organisations do not invest and prioritise psychosocial support for staff, the consequences are vast:

> workers suffering from the effects of stress are likely to be less efficient and less effective in carrying out their assigned tasks. They become poor decision makers and they may behave in ways that place themselves or other members of the team at risk or disrupt the effective functioning of the team. They are more likely to have accidents or to become ill. A consequence for humanitarian agencies is that staff stress and burnout may impede recruitment and retention of qualified staff, increase health care costs, compromise safety and security of staff and create legal liabilities.
>
> (Antares, 2012, p. 7)

If something goes wrong the cost can be substantial. A prime example of this is the Steven Patrick Dennis versus the Norwegian Refugee Council (NRC) case. In June 2012 Dennis, a Canadian, was kidnapped and shot in the thigh in Dadaab refugee camp, Kenya. Three other NRC staff were also kidnapped and the driver was killed. They were held for four days, after which they were rescued by Kenyan authorities and a local militia. Dennis' case of negligence to his duty of care against the NRC was successful, and resulted in a substantial compensation payout. Dennis was awarded damages for both psychological and physical injury. This momentous case has been described as a 'wake-up call' for the humanitarian sector.

There is no excuse for organisations not to have clear duty of care policies in order, as there are several psychosocial support guidelines that are widely available, including: the Antares Framework (2012); IASC MHPSS Guidelines (2007); and the Sphere Guidebook (2011). People in Aid published *Approaches to Staff Care in International NGOs* (People in Aid & InterHealth, 2009), where 20 NGOs were interviewed about their staff care policies. The survey found that practices were inconsistent at best, and only one-third of organisations had a specific staff care policy. The inconsistent staff care in the humanitarian sector was reflected in the data and comments that I gathered from my own research:

> I've worked in the humanitarian sector for 15 years now and I've never worked for an organisation that offered appropriate access to psychosocial support. I've always had to seek care on my own.
>
> (Samad, Bangladesh)

> We have an employee assistance programme (EAP), which has worked well when it has been used, although take up has been low. Since changing the referral system, the take up has been better.
>
> (Lukas, Austria)

> My organisation launched a program to detect early signs of burn out and trauma among their humanitarian workers. This has been really helpful.
>
> (Aamir, Yemen)

The Inter-Agency Standing Committee (IASC, 2007) states six key actions in preventing and managing problems in mental health and psychosocial wellbeing among staff and volunteers: ensure the availability of a concrete plan to protect and promote staff wellbeing for specific emergencies; prepare staff for their jobs and for the emergency context; facilitate a healthy working environment; address potential work-related stressors; ensure access to health care and psychosocial support for staff; provide support to staff who have experienced or witnessed extreme events (critical incidents, potentially traumatic events).

Ripple effect of trauma

I have attended too many meetings where individuals become statistics, and where these statistics become minimalised and perceived as one-dimensional. Most people recover naturally from trauma exposure after a few weeks, although for some the symptoms continue and the employee could develop mental health problems including post-traumatic stress, anxiety, depression and compassion fatigue (Huddlestone, Paton & Stephens, 2006). Statistics focus on the individual who is suffering, but the reality of affected numbers is far greater. Trauma has a ripple effect; it does not just impact the individual, but also their families, friends, teams, colleagues, the project and quality of work, and the organisation.

I believe one factor for organisations to remain resilient to shock is strong leadership; being able to sit with the discomfort of really listening to someone's experiences, however distressing. As Ramalingham noted, in his book *Aid on the Edge of Chaos*, good leadership calls for a focus on strength rather than power (Ramalingham, 2013). Aideen Lucey, an organisational consultant, shared with me the idea of 'emotion as intelligence' rather than 'emotional intelligence'. She noted that:

> the expression of emotions in organisations can be a source of intelligence about the work. Difficult emotions and experiences are thought about as having a meaning connected to the purpose of the organisation. Seen this way, stress, and its particular manifestations, become a communication about the work rather than a symptom of pathology in the individual worker.
>
> (Lucey, 2017)

The fact is that aid workers are at significant risk of psychological ill-health, as shown by the research discussed below. The effects of cumulative stress and other less 'quantifiable' outcomes of trauma are not as clearly researched or documented. The more accessible statistics make for difficult reading:

- The *Aid Worker Security Report* highlighted that in 2016, 158 major attacks against aid operations occurred, in which 101 aid workers were killed, 98 wounded and 89 kidnapped (Stoddard, Harmer & Czwarno, 2017, p. 1).
- Since 2006, kidnapping of aid workers has increased by 350 per cent (Stoddard, Harmer & DiDomenico, 2009) and is considered to be the most used form of violence against aid workers (Schreter & Harmer, 2013).
- Between 55 and 78 per cent of aid workers experience at least one seriously frightening or disturbing incident during the course of their work and between 19 and 33 per cent of humanitarian workers report feeling that their life is in danger (Connorton, Perry, Hemenway & Miller, 2011).
- There is a significant body of evidence to demonstrate that workers directly exposed to traumatic events, including transportation disasters, physical attack, shootings, harassment and accidents, during the course of their work have an increased risk of developing PTSD, major depression, anxiety and/or drug dependency (Breslau, 1998).

- A study that examined the mental health of national humanitarian aid workers in northern Uganda concluded that over 50 per cent of workers experienced five or more categories of traumatic events. Additionally, respondents reported symptom levels associated with high risk for depression (68 per cent), anxiety disorders (53 per cent) and PTSD (26 per cent), and between one-quarter and one-half of respondents reported symptom levels associated with burnout (Ager et al., 2012).
- A recent longitudinal study indicated humanitarians are at increased risk for depression, anxiety and burnout during deployment and after returning; aid workers also had lower levels of life satisfaction compared with pre-deployment levels, even months after returning from the field (Cardozo et al., 2012).

These figures are likely to be greater, particularly for national staff, where legal procedures and the cultural implications of discussing mental ill-health can make reporting more difficult.

> Despite its ubiquitous presence, whether in crisis zones such as Syria, Yemen or the Congo, or day-to-day existence in both the developing and industrialised worlds, trauma often remains largely unrecognised and untreated. It is the same in the humanitarian sector. As a psychologist working for 30 years in the aid and humanitarian sectors, I have observed my own vulnerability – and that of others.
>
> (O'Donnell, 2017)

A survey of 113 aid workers across five humanitarian organisations concluded that approximately 30 per cent of staff reported significant symptoms of PTSD (Eriksson, Kemp, Gorsuch, Hoke & Foy, 2012). In comparison, the National Comorbidity Survey Replication (NCS-R), conducted between February 2001 and April 2003, comprised interviews of a nationally representative sample of 9,282 Americans aged 18 years and older. PTSD was assessed among 5,692 participants, using DSM-IV criteria. The NCS-R estimated the lifetime prevalence of PTSD among adult Americans to be 6.8 per cent (Adshed & Ferris, 2007). Therefore, aid workers are experiencing trauma levels much greater than the national average, and more aligned with individuals exposed to war: about 30 per cent of the men and women who have spent time in more recent war zones experience PTSD (Iribarren, Prolo, Neagos & Chiappelli, 2005), and to individuals exposed to terrorist attacks, for example in the 9/11 US terrorist attack on the twin towers in New York, the prevalence of PTSD for those actually in the building, or injured, equated to 30 per cent (Hamblen & Slone, 2016).

The changing face of aid work

Humanitarian aid is changing, and there are many reasons why this is so. Due to changes in global conflict patterns aid workers are becoming more entangled with foreign and military policy, which can create a perception that aid workers are no longer neutral entities:

> unfortunately, a priori decisions to react and harden against attack create humanitarian fortresses that further separate aid workers from the populations they assist and help to create a situation in which fear threatens to eclipse the humanitarian imagination. These mechanisms may save lives, but at what cost?
>
> (Fast, 2014, p. 26)

Humanitarian aid is a growing industry and there is an ever-increasing demand for a greater number of people to be deployed to volatile and dangerous environments. Protracted conflicts causing forced displacement and adding to global migration movements are set to continue. There has also been an increase in the rise of terrorist attacks and natural disasters affecting a greater number of people (Stoddard et al., 2009). In turn,

> striking at aid operations can be a means to destabilise and delegitimise the current order, punish or extort local populations, raise [perpetrators] visibility and political profile, or simply obtain economic assets in the form of goods, cash, vehicles or ransoms.
>
> (Fast, 2014)

All of the above factors are contributing to aid work becoming more volatile and unpredictable.

Christoph Hensch shared with me his personal account of a direct attack on aid workers at an International Committee of the Red Cross (ICRC) surgical hospital in Novye Atagi, Chechnya on 17 December 1996. Only a few months earlier, the ICRC had opened a hospital in order to care for those who were wounded by the Chechen conflict. Christoph was the appointed Head of Office at the time. Six international staff were murdered and, even though Christoph was shot, he survived.

> It was an unprecedented and unprovoked act of violence against the organisation and its workers.... My journey and that of the organisation seemed to move on parallel lines, and as in a true parallel, the lines did not touch except at certain specific events.... Very little time was spent walking next to each other, supporting each other. Individuals have to live their journey by themselves.

Christoph went on to describe how he felt the organisation resisted hearing his voice: 'like an invisible barrier going up ... as if people do not want to look at this side of the humanitarian action coin'. He felt a great deal of anger towards the organisation, which unfortunately led him to hand in his resignation (Hensch, 2016).

Hensch felt that 'the biggest failure that occurred along the way was the inability to establish a fruitful process where both the individual and the community co-created a healing journey'. He proposes an integrated approach to recovering from trauma and stress, made up of four components:

1 objective support: access to professional services;
2 systemic environment: organisations need comprehensive policies, procedures and operating standards that reflect the duty of care for staff;
3 organisational culture: the ethos and values of an organisation to incorporate psychosocial and peer support;
4 subjective experience: identifying and acting upon the personal needs of the staff member.

> The invisible costs that individual humanitarian workers are paying can be immense: working in insecure environments and experiencing and witnessing acts of violence and the suffering they cause can have adverse and devastating impacts.... It took many years to make sense of what happened to me and my colleagues on that fateful day twenty years ago, and to overcome the effects of PTSD. From my perspective, the initial experience of being shot was a trigger to a much longer experience of recovery, which was much more prolonged and painful than it needed to be.
>
> (Hensch, 2016)

The scars of wisdom

My experience of suffering PTSD was over 20 years ago. Alongside Christoph Hensch (ICRC) and Jon Barden (a contractor working for DFID), all three of our stories are shared within this book. Not only do we share the scars of PTSD, but we also feel passionate about sharing our stories, so that individuals and organisations can co-create a protective, supportive and healing community. In a world where humanitarian principles are becoming increasingly harder to hold on to, we need to offer ourselves, our staff and our organisations, the humanitarian principles of humanity, neutrality, impartiality and independence.

No one should fall through the net of psychosocial support, and no one should suffer with PTSD for years. It is accepted that trauma is a psychological risk hazard to aid work, and research is highlighting that this risk is increasing, therefore it is imperative organisations implement a trauma management programme into their duty of care policies, and that there is a clear pathway of psychosocial support for all staff throughout their employment.

As Report the Abuse enabled survivors of sexual violence to step forward and have a voice, we need to continue to break the silence of trauma injuries, create a safe container for people to speak out, normalise the impact of trauma, implement best-practice processes and enable individuals to recover well and in a timely manner. Having worked in the public, private and charity sector, the charity sector is lagging behind in offering psychosocial support services to staff, which goes against the grain of its values and ethos. Therefore, individuals and organisations need to have a greater awareness and knowledge of how to protect 'the carers' of our world, so they can remain resilient and continue to carry out the great work that they do.

Trauma and psychological distress become part of the ebb and flow of life. We can recover from acute stress and trauma injury, with the appropriate help and support. It may leave scars, but if processed those scars become engraved with understanding and wisdom. That wisdom can be used to help others in their recovery. The whisper of that wisdom comes across in every personal story shared in this book.

2   The physiology of trauma

The mechanics of trauma

I'm so tired and I cannot sleep,
As my fears all surface and drag me in deep.
The darkness and anguish hit me between the eyes.
All those memories I desperately try to deny.
The dark shadows follow me around every day.
Those thoughts of despair I can't shake away.

> (One verse from a poem the author wrote after suffering PTSD)

I was attacked in my early twenties and spent several episodes in therapy trying to manage, what I came to know, many years later, as post-traumatic stress disorder (PTSD).

When the emergency services found me I was slumped against a wall down a dark alley, unconscious. As I came to in the ambulance I began to make out blurred faces and hazy lights; everything was out of focus. Voices were fading in and out. Someone was holding my hand. 'What's your name, what's your name?' I heard the words over and over again, but they took some time to register with me. I realised then that I didn't know who I was. *What was my name? I had no idea!*

I had gone to the aid of another young woman who was being attacked down an alleyway. At the time I didn't even think about my own safety. Was this in itself a trauma response, or perhaps it was conditioning from my childhood? What led me to put myself at risk to help someone else? My recovery led me down the path of trauma awareness, and it was during this process that I learnt how to take care of myself in a healthy way.

How would you respond when faced with a traumatic incident? Would you recognise the symptoms of trauma and know where to go for specialist support? Could you offer forensic and medical guidance to a colleague who had just been raped? If you don't feel confident in answering these questions then further trauma training is crucial, otherwise you are putting yourself and others at risk. I see so many aid workers deploying to high-risk environments unprepared for what they might be exposed to. I will continue to repeat in this book the importance of trauma awareness, stress and resilience training as a vital component in preparing aid workers deploying to high-risk environments (or those managing traumatic material, even from a safe distance).

What is trauma?

'Traumatic events overwhelm the ordinary systems of care that give people a sense of control, connection, and meaning' (Herman, 1997, p. 33). Trauma is a deeply distressing experience and can impact an individual at their core, in mind, body and spirit. Often individuals associate trauma with major events such as war, road traffic accidents, kidnapping and hostage-taking, sexual violent crime, robbery, assault, serious accidents, childhood physical and sexual abuse and natural disasters. Individuals can also experience trauma symptoms from domestic violence, a difficult relationship breakup, adoption, bullying at school or in the workplace, displacement, childhood neglect and emotional abuse, harassment, being a target of stalking, losing a job, witnessing or being indirectly exposed to traumatic material, and traumatic bereavements (sudden death, i.e. suicide). Trauma covers a vast spectrum of events. How an individual is impacted is also influenced by their perception of the event. For example, when I worked at Transport for London, I often heard comments questioning why a train operator who experienced a 'near miss' compared to an 'actual suicide' on the line was off sick or in trauma recovery. In that moment of seeing someone on the track, regardless of whether the individual is hit by the train or not, the train operator will experience the same physiological trauma reactions and may need time to recover from the shock. Also, until a thorough assessment is carried out we will not know how that individual has been impacted, what support structures they have in their life, what other stress factors they may be experiencing and what previous incidents may have been triggered. All of these factors will dictate how someone is impacted.

Furthermore, individuals can experience trauma symptoms vicariously. This is also called 'secondary trauma', which can be triggered by living with someone who is traumatised or carrying out a role where you are indirectly listening to or witnessing traumatic material. Journalists, therapists, aid workers, medical staff, social workers and care workers can all be exposed to vicarious trauma. Likewise, office staff can be exposed vicariously to trauma. This was highlighted in the Ebola response. Aid workers that were exposed to stories remotely started to experience trauma symptoms and requested psychological support.

The survival response

As I stated at the beginning of this chapter, what might you do if you are confronted with a traumatic incident? Would you confront the situation, as I did, or would you run away, call for help or freeze on the spot? The three main reactions to trauma are 'Fight', 'Flight' or 'Freeze'. The fourth, less acknowledged, reaction is 'Fawn' (appease). To describe all four reactions I will use an example of a team of staff who experience their manager as a bully. Some staff will become rebellious, try to 'Fight' the bully, or take out a grievance. Others will want to leave, taking up the 'Flight' reaction. Some staff may feel 'Frozen', unsure what to do, unable to act. And the fourth reaction, 'Fawn', may result in staff wanting to please all parties, as if turning a blind eye to what is occurring and pretend everything is fine. We see clear examples of this in the Jimmy Savile case, where so many people directly witnessed or suspected that Jimmy Savile was sexually abusing children and didn't say anything. This is a trauma reaction, as these individuals are often frightened of the consequences of speaking up. In sexual violent crime 'Freeze' is often the most common response. When an individual feels 'over-powered', freeze may seem like the only option available.

Unfortunately, as humans we start to criticise our response. Compared to animals who can shake off the trauma and get on with the next day, humans start to berate and judge themselves, for 'getting it wrong' or 'not being good enough'. The four survival reactions are needed; they may save our lives! We will not necessarily be able to override our response and may react differently in different scenarios. Individuals who have been through intensive military training or trauma exposure training may be able to control their survival reactions. The problem starts when we can no longer return to 'normal'. Resilience is about 'bouncing back' after distressing experiences, but due to the impact of trauma on the brain this is not always possible. Trauma experiences change our neurobiology and brain patterning.

How is the brain impacted by trauma?

The simplest way to describe how the brain is impacted is to imagine the brain in three sections: the reptilian, limbic and neocortex. This is often referred to as the triune brain (MacLean, 1990).

The triune brain

- Reptilian: imagine this as the central part of the brain, the part of the brain that is connected to the brain stem. This part of the brain is often compared to a reptile's brain. It represents the survival functions, including functions such as breathing, eating, balance and temperature.

- Limbic: the limbic is the mid-brain. It is often referred to as our emotional or mammalian brain.
- Prefrontal cortex: imagine the neocortex as the outer layer of the brain. This holds the executive functions of the brain, such as: analytical and rational thinking, language and decision-making abilities.

When we are highly stressed or traumatised the prefrontal cortex part of the brain goes offline. Therefore, it is hard to have a rational conversation with someone who is stressed, as the thinking and language part of the brain becomes disconnected. When stressed we function from the emotional brain, a combination of the limbic and reptilian brain. Professor Steve Peters describes this as our 'chimp brain' (Peters, 2012), when functioning from this part of the brain we are more emotional and reactive.

Other parts of the brain I will describe which are connected to the trauma response include the thalamus, amygdala, hypothalamus and the hippocampus.

- Thalamus: the thalamus is often referred to as the information gateway to the brain, as most of our sensory input is translated through the thalamus. If it signals potential threat the thalamus will send a message to the amygdala.
- Amygdala: this is our fire alarm system. It warns us when we perceive threat. The amygdala consists of two almond-shaped structures that lie deep in the limbic brain.
- Hypothalamus (below the thalamus) controls the autonomic nervous system (ANS). If it is alerted to danger it demands the ANS to release hormones such as adrenaline, noradrenaline and cortisol, activating the body into 'Fight', 'Flight', 'Freeze' or 'Fawn' states.

    - Sympathetic nervous system: this is related to the fight and flight response as it increases the heart rate and breathing, creates a rush of energy to the muscles, and suppresses any non-essential systems. Creating a state of hyper-arousal, generating energy and being ready for action.
    - Parasympathetic nervous system: this is associated with the freeze response as it decreases autonomic activation, can produce shaking and trembling and a sense of shutting down and total collapse. Developing a state of hypo-arousal, often resulting in total exhaustion.

- Hippocampus: when information is fully processed our memories get stored in the hippocampus, which can be referred to as the 'filing cabinet of the brain'. The hippocampus also creates a sense of meaning and time between events, therefore creating a past, present and future.

- Dentate nucleus: this is a cluster of neurons that enable information to be processed and stored in the hippocampus. Gordon Turnbull (2011) refers to this as the 'fuse', as these neurones can be damaged or even destroyed when an individual experiences trauma or acute stress, blowing a 'fuse' to protect the brain from extreme overwhelm. Therefore, when these neurons are damaged we can no longer process and store information in our filing system (the hippocampus). Research has found that these neurons can repair themselves, which takes approximately 30 days (Manji, Drevets & Chaney, 2001). This could help us to understand why it is recommended that the 'trauma processing' part of therapy does not take place for the first four weeks after an incident, as our brain is naturally trying to restore itself.

The brain needs to process whether we are in danger before information is filed in the hippocampus. Due to this process we could be viewed as having a 'negative brain bias' (Siegel, 2010). When we feel threatened we often think the worst, before we can reassure ourselves that we are OK. For example, I was lying in the grass on a summer's day and I felt something wriggle under my arm. My immediate response was to jump up and remove myself from danger, my thalamus and amygdala became activated, as I felt my heart rate increase. I then tentatively looked back at the spot on the grass and realised it was a twig, rather than a snake! This allowed my system to calm down, process the incident and file it as a memory in my hippocampus. A traumatic event does not always allow the brain to process the memory and therefore it can continue to be retriggered and activate the survival response. On the positive side, Siegel explains the neuroplasticity of the brain, which means we can reformat the brain from reliving a trauma into recovery, and even adults who have suffered PTSD for over ten years, whether through war or severe childhood developmental traumas, can recover with the right specialist help.

Douglas Bremner, a physician and researcher from the United States, explored the impact of trauma on the brain: 'patients with post-traumatic stress disorder (PTSD) showing smaller hippocampal and anterior cingulate volumes, increased amygdala function, and decreased medial prefrontal/anterior cingulate function' (Bremner, 2006, p. 445). A smaller hippocampus depletes our memory, an increase in amygdala function will keep us in a state of alert, and a decreased prefrontal (neocortex) will make it difficult to think logically and act responsibly. Therefore, it becomes harder to make decisions, concentrate and stay focused when we experience acute stress or trauma. Bremner identified that army veterans with

PTSD exhibited an 8 per cent reduction in the volume of their right hippo-campus compared with veterans who suffered no such symptoms. He also recognised that Romanian orphans suffering from PTSD had significantly smaller right hippocampal volumes (Bremner et al., 1995). This has a detrimental impact on brain development and the ability to learn. These children are often labelled as having 'problem behaviours', pathologised and prescribed medication, when actually specialist trauma counselling may be the best treatment for them.

I had direct experience of this when I worked in an orphanage in China. I could see first-hand how these toddlers were impacted by developmental trauma and lack of healthy attachments to care-givers; they often presented with extreme behaviours of the Fight, Flight, Freeze states, including hitting out, clinging on to me for dear life, or skirting around the edge of the room, too terrified to come close. They had no idea how to form healthy attachments to other human beings and their brain development had been severely impacted by the horrific experiences they had been exposed to so early on in their lives. Adele, an aid worker, after returning from a deployment in a Romanian orphanage, tentatively expressed, 'I was afraid of the children, they were like wild animals'. She felt so guilty for feeling this way, and had not been able to express her honest feelings about this until attending therapy. This is a normal survival reaction and when Adele began to understand the mechanics of trauma she could start her recovery process. It was the guilt that had kept her 'locked in' to the awful trauma memories she was exposed to.

When I arrived at the hospital I spent the night projectile vomiting and squinting each hour as a torch was shone in my eyes. I had a black eye, fractured jawbone and concussion. A haze of nurses came to seek me out, whispering behind their hands, 'she's the one who went to help the woman being attacked'.

In the six months that followed I was frightened to go out and often felt paranoid. I would only venture out when I had to. I felt I was at risk, and that someone was about to jump out on me and attack me. Sleep was the worst. I couldn't sleep for several months. I had constant flashbacks of the event and intrusive thoughts. I had been an outgoing and sociable individual, but after the incident I lost all my confidence. I wanted to crack the shell of isolation that was suffocating me, but I didn't know how to reach out to people. I was uncomfortable in my own skin. I felt shattered, fragmented and broken. I felt exhausted and completely spent. I believed I was going mad.

When traumatised clients come to see me for the first time I often hear them ask, 'am I going mad?', 'am I crazy?' The array of symptoms one experiences after a trauma can feel overwhelming and crazy-making. Below I will endeavour to explain the symptoms of trauma.

Common trauma symptoms

Babette Rothschild, a psychotherapist specialising in trauma and author of *The Body Remembers*, notes:

> Trauma continues to intrude with visual, auditory, and/or other somatic reality on the lives of its victims. Again and again, they relive the life-threatening experiences they have suffered, reacting in mind and body as though such events were still occurring.
>
> (Rothschild, 2000, p. 6)

- Flashbacks: flashbacks and intrusive thoughts can appear when we are least expecting them to, it may seem they come 'out of the blue', although something will have triggered them, whether it be a sound, smell or place reminding us of the traumatic or distressing memory.

Dabor, who lives and works in South Sudan for a large NGO, described how 'every time I heard a loud bang I was frightened. I became jumpy and on edge when exposed to loud noises. This would bring everything I was desperately trying not to think about flooding back to my mind'.

- Palpitations and panic attacks: our heart and lungs have to work really hard to pump the blood and oxygen around the body at speed. This increases our heart rate, which can lead to palpitations and/or raised blood pressure. I have known individuals to be rushed to an Accident & Emergency (A&E) Unit thinking they are having a heart attack. After receiving the all-clear on test results they were told it is stress related. This is how serious physical symptoms related to stress can become.
- Concentration and memory impairment: as mentioned earlier, the pre-frontal cortex goes offline and the hippocampal functioning is impaired, causing difficulty with concentration and memory.
- Difficulty sleeping: sleep is often the first thing to deteriorate after a distressing or traumatic incident. This can also lead to dreams or nightmares that disturb our sleep, often with the theme of 'not feeling safe'.

James, an aid worker who was kidnapped, described how his sleep was disturbed:

> About three weeks after the incident, when I did get to sleep, I would have very vivid dreams about the most horrendous mass

casualty events involving means of transport (air, road and train crashes). Around fifty percent of the time these would involve my family or friends as the victims, the rest of the time the victims were strangers.

- Changes to appetite: some individuals start to binge eat, eating unhealthy foods. The liver produces glucose to inject us with an energy boost. Therefore we can be drawn to eat sugary foods. Others may lose their appetite altogether and feel nauseous.
- Stomach problems: our bladder, bowels and digestive system start to shut down when we are traumatised or acutely stressed. Initially we may feel the need to go to the toilet more often than normal or feel 'butterflies' in our stomach. Over a period of time individuals can start to experience stomach issues such as Irritable Bowel Syndrome (IBS) or stomach ulcers.
- Emotional outbursts: some individuals will experience unexpected moments of bursting into tears, or becoming irritable and angry towards those closest to them.
- Paranoia: as our senses will be on hyper-alert, we will be watching out for threat and danger. This can result in some individuals feeling paranoid and on edge.
- Numbness: some individuals will feel a sense of 'not being there', as if watching the world go on inside a TV set or feeling slightly removed and disconnected from what is going on.
- Anxiety and depression: it is common to feel a great deal of anxiety when distressed. This makes it hard for individuals to relax. This also consumes a great deal of energy, which can then lead to feelings of depression.
- Temperature changes: the blood moves towards the large muscles, getting ready for the action. The blood moves away from the skin, causing hot or cold flushes. This is also a life-saving action, as it will help the blood clot if we are injured.
- Shaking: some individuals may experience shaking directly after a traumatic event. Adrenaline pumps through the muscles to prepare us for action.

When I arrived at the hospital the medical staff suspected I had a fractured skull. I remember desperately holding onto the bars on the side of my hospital bed trying to stop myself shaking so that the X-ray would work. Trauma is held in the body, and I believe that shaking after an event is our body's natural way to release the trauma.

Under threat, massive amounts of energy are mobilised in readiness for self-defence via the fight, flight, and freeze responses. Once safe, animals spontaneously 'discharge' this excess energy through involuntary movements including shaking, trembling, and deep spontaneous breaths. This discharge process resets the autonomic nervous system, restoring equilibrium.

(Levine, 1997)

During trauma treatment I have experienced clients shaking or experiencing tingling throughout their body, as if energy is trying to shift the trauma on a cellular level.

- Avoidance: individuals may be inclined to avoid certain places or events that will remind them of the distressing incident.
- Immune system: our immune system is not needed in an emergency situation and, similar to the stomach, shuts down. In the longer term this will make it much harder for our body to fight off infection and illness. Fibromyalgia and chronic fatigue can also be related to the trauma or acute stress response.
- Increase in alcohol or drug usage: some individuals will start to self-medicate, whether through alcohol or drugs, as a way to supress emotions and induce sleep. This will need to be monitored, as the risk is that it could become a crutch and develop into an unhealthy coping strategy.
- Isolation: if there is shame linked to the incident some individuals may end up isolating themselves and withdrawing from social connections. In extreme situations this can lead to the breakdown of relationships.
- Negative thinking: often self-berating thoughts of 'I'm not good enough', 'I failed', 'I am to blame', 'I am weak' start to multiply in our minds. There is a great deal of shame or guilt associated with traumatic events. This is created from the human need to be in control. It is more comfortable for us for us to believe we could have changed the outcome, than to accept that we were powerless to change the outcome. This often becomes the focus of trauma therapy.
- Exhaustion: all of the above symptoms take their toll on the body, therefore it is not surprising that individuals can feel exhausted.

Abdul, an aid worker who witnessed a car bombing, described his symptoms as:

mental exhaustion, inability to think clearly, memory loss, lack of productivity, feeling overwhelmed with work, physical pain (cramps in my lower stomach), inability to relax. Following the security incident I was very distressed: stress while travelling and inability to sleep.

Some individuals do not evidence any trauma symptoms after a traumatic event, and those that do will experience their own personal combination of the above symptoms. Most people recover from trauma naturally, within four to six weeks. It is also important to keep in mind that some individuals will experience a 'delayed trauma' response. This can happen months or even years after an event.

The Greek translation of the word trauma means 'wound' (*Oxford English Dictionary*, 1999). Trauma is the invisible wound of the mind. As I ventured back to university for the first time after I was attacked I had my first panic attack. Obviously not knowing at the time what was wrong with me, it was terrifying. I couldn't breathe and I had a strong urge to run. But where would I run to? There was nowhere I could go to get away from me. On the way home I bumped into a friend who said, 'oh you look OK, I thought you would look so much worse'. Bear in mind that after a traumatic incident, individuals are highly sensitive to comments from friends, colleagues and managers. As a therapist I find that clients often get fixated on what someone said to them or did after the incident that felt unsupportive. This can become the main focus of the therapy work. I found my friend's comment insensitive, she had no idea what I was feeling beyond my physical appearance, that I felt broken and shattered into tiny pieces and uncertain if I was ever going to be able to put myself back together again.

It took me over a month before I had one good night's sleep. I would resist reliving the 'moment I was knocked unconscious' in my dreams, and therefore automatically woke up. Until one night I was so exhausted I couldn't stop myself nodding off. That night *I felt the full force of his fist as it hit my head*. I then woke to the sound of 'white noise'. I remember getting out of bed and walking around the house, trying to work out where the noise was coming from, until it dawned on me that the noise was in my head.

The main focus of trauma treatments is to move the processing of the traumatic material from the amygdala (the fire alarm system of the brain) to the hippocampus (the filing system of the brain); to make meaning, to create a narrative, to find a new perspective that is less derogatory of self, to reduce the symptoms of trauma and to find a way to regulate the body back to a relaxed state. Once the memory becomes processed and stored in the hippocampus we have more control over it, and we can choose when or if to view it. When it is stuck on replay and activating the amygdala, we feel as if we are back in the trauma memory, and it controls us. Kamill, a journalist, describes how he felt after trauma counselling:

As with any troubling event we always learn and take something from it. The treatment I received allowed me to do that and rather than just blocking it out and trying to forget about it I've been able to move forward and am stronger for it. I would advise anyone suffering from trauma symptoms not to suffer in silence, the nature of aid work means we're regularly exposed to traumatic events. I will never forget the things I witnessed in Sierra Leone. When I think about them now it still makes me sad, but I'm now in control of those thoughts and feelings rather than them controlling me.

There is a great deal written about post-traumatic growth (Joseph, 2011), by working through a trauma we can become stronger and some individuals go on to use their experiences to help others. I find working with trauma inspiring, not only because of witnessing the human spirit to survive, but also because of the privilege to travel such difficult terrain with an individual who is suffering to a path of greater resilience, self-compassion and traumatic growth.

How do we learn to process trauma that has become stuck in our body? How do we oil the mechanisms of our brain and body so they can work in unison again? If symptoms have persisted over four weeks, unhealthy coping strategies may have become ingrained. The next chapter explores treating trauma; the support vehicles needed to recover from trauma and PTSD.

Tristan Clements, Regional Risk Director for World Vision, shared his story of being caught up in a violent ambush during a field visit in Sudan's volatile Darfur region, in 2007. Two of his colleagues were shot in the back of the vehicle, and although they were all physically and psychologically wounded, they miraculously walked away with their lives. In his blog he describes how he was impacted:

for the first three years after the attack, it was in my head every single day, in visceral detail. The sight of a white Land Cruiser was a visual trigger for me (unfortunate in our industry) and would take me right back to my seat when the bullets started coming through. I had long hours lying awake in my cabin in northern PNG in 2008 while huge thunderstorms crashed overhead, heart-rate elevated; diving in a head-long run from my shower in Colombo in early 2009 as explosions sounded outside only to discover they were wedding fireworks beyond my hotel window; throwing my then-fiancée to the ground when a loud bang sounded nearby in rural Australia. Despite having re-told the story more than a dozen times, years later I would still find my chest tight and my fingers shaking trying to recount what had happened to friends; even though I 'felt' emotionally calm, my body betrayed me.

(Clements, 2010)

3 Treating trauma

Support vehicles of recovery

I thought I was doing well for the first few weeks and managed to switch off everything, but slowly as the weeks passed the intrusive thoughts from my trip kept popping into my head. They'd happen at the most inappropriate times – on the train, on the treadmill, having dinner with friends, clothes shopping, you name it, the images kept reappearing. The most embarrassing was in a team meeting where I simply burst into tears for no apparent reason. It wasn't just the intrusive thoughts either, it was that coupled with the sleepless nights, a loss of appetite, anger, guilt, irritability and just a feeling of being completely exhausted. As an avid gym-goer I couldn't work out why I was feeling so tired when my routine was exactly the same as before.

(Kamil, Italy)

What are trauma specialist treatments?

On this journey of trauma recovery what are the *support vehicles of recovery* for treating trauma? What are the different therapeutic models, and how do they work? As I mentioned in the previous chapter, I suffered PTSD in my early twenties, and as it took me a long time to find specialist trauma support, I am passionate about enabling individuals to find the best quality trauma support, and quickly. The longer someone suffers from trauma-related symptoms the more complex their recovery process can become, as many individuals develop unhealthy coping strategies such as self-medication, alcohol or drug use, over-working, changes in diet, self-harming, breakdown of relationships, isolation, aggression and risky behaviours, all of which can deepen and further entrench their original symptoms. Although most people recover from trauma naturally, if symptoms persist for over four to six weeks then specialist trauma therapy may be helpful.

There are several different approaches to psychotherapy, which can be confusing if you are searching for a therapist. It is important to be aware that some therapists will state that they work with trauma, but will not have had specialist trauma training. In basic terms there are three main approaches to psychotherapy: Psychodynamic, Humanistic and Cognitive Behavioural therapies. I would describe myself as an Integrative therapist, and therefore I work with a combination of these approaches. Additional trauma specialist models include: Trauma-Focused Cognitive Behavioural Therapy (TF-CBT), Eye Movement Desensitisation Reprocessing (EMDR), Narrative Exposure Therapy (NET) and Sensorimotor Therapy. There are other models of working with trauma but further research is needed into the efficacy of these various approaches. All trauma approaches aim to help the client to create a trauma narrative, find meaning in the event, and reduce the trauma symptoms, whether through talking, drawing, play or writing. Most trauma models follow a three-step treatment programme: stabilisation, processing and integration (Herman, 1997). I will explain these stages in the case studies that follow.

When searching for a trauma specialist therapist, ideally seek someone who has completed the main body of training, has gained accreditation and has carried out *additional* trauma specialist training. The National Institute for Health and Care Excellence (NICE), the World Health Organization (WHO) and the American Psychological Association (APA) recommend two specialist trauma models: TF-CBT and EMDR. I will briefly explain both of these models and offer a more detailed case study from each approach. There is a vast amount of research showing the successful integration of using these approaches globally, relevant materials have been translated into different languages, and techniques have been culturally adapted (see Chapter 7). Trauma Aid UK and Europe have offered *pro bono* training in EMDR to appropriately qualified practitioners in over 30 countries, in order to enable and provide good quality trauma care in countries that have little, if any, access to specialist trauma treatment.

EMDR: how does it work?

Francine Shapiro, PhD, Senior Research Fellow at the Mental Research Institute, Palo Alto, California and Executive Director of the EMDR Institute, California, is the 'originator and developer' of EMDR (Shapiro, 1989). Since then, EMDR has been adapted and reworked based on the research and contributions of therapists and researchers the world over. Initially used as a treatment with Vietnam veterans who weren't recovering, it has since proven successful in treating various other presentations, including anxiety, phobias, addictions, depression, complicated grief, abuse and performance anxiety. The unique feature in EMDR therapy is that it uses bilateral stimulation (BLS) whilst processing the distressing memory (Shapiro, 2005). BLS can be conducted by following the therapist's hand as it moves from left to right, watching a light bar, or tapping. The same can also be achieved through listening to alternating bilateral tones or holding buzzers. The BLS alleviates negative cognitions, negative emotion and unpleasant physical sensations associated with a traumatic or distressing memory. An important concept of EMDR is the 'Adaptive Information Processing (AIP)' theory (Parnell, 2007). This means the client begins to reformulate and update dysfunctional self-beliefs, and replaces them with positive self-reflecting beliefs. Therefore, EMDR promotes our innate healing process and reformats dysfunctional information to functional, so that it becomes *adaptive information processing*. 'Just as the river flows to the sea and the body heals the wound, EMDR clears the trauma and brings integration and wholeness' (Parnell, 2007, p. 6). In discussing EMDR, Professor Gordon Turnbull states: 'Therapists and patients were reporting that problems that had been resistant to years of psychotherapy were being resolved in a very short amount of time – sometimes within a few sessions' (Turnbull, 2011). In my experience of working within the field of trauma for over 15 years I have never witnessed such a powerful and successful way of working with traumatised and anxious clients: 'EMDR works effectively and helps the client return to work quickly and safely after a traumatic event' (Dunkley & Claridge, 2012). The EMDR protocol sets out an eight-phase treatment plan:

1   client history and treatment planning;
2   preparation;
3   assessment;
4   desensitisation;
5   installation;
6   body scan;
7   closure;
8   re-evaluation (Shapiro, 2001, 2004).

The case study below presents a first-hand experience of how EMDR works.

Case study 1 (EMDR)

I came to therapy after experiencing trauma symptoms following a trip to Turkey where I witnessed a violent failed *coup d'état*. In spite of having triggered the emergency/security protocol while in Turkey, upon my return I was not offered counselling to debrief the incident. The incident was considered important as the executive director and other senior managers were being briefed on my situation twice daily while still in Turkey. In that sense, I did not feel my organisation supported me in dealing with the fall outs of the incident. I had to request for help through HR and it was almost two months before I was able to see a counsellor.

Through this experience, I wondered whether other colleagues who may not have been as comfortable going to see a therapist, or afraid of the stigma attached to doing so, would have requested the support. I believe my organisation should make post-incident debriefing mandatory, as part of the incident management protocol. It would help those who may need a little bit more encouragement to seek help.

EMDR addressed my PTSD symptoms effectively. It enabled me to understand why I was reacting the way I was, rather than being left to feel weak or stupid for experiencing such distress. It has now been over six months since the treatment and I have not experienced any symptoms in that time. The changes in how I felt and the reduction of the symptoms I was experiencing was quick. I now feel that the issue is resolved and this is not something I will continue to carry with me.

(Chris, aid worker)

Session one

Preparation/assessment/resourcing

The initial stage of trauma therapy, often referred to as 'stabilisation', includes a detailed assessment, building the therapist–client relationship, and introducing techniques so that clients can learn to relax and ground themselves when dealing with the more difficult feelings that may come up during the trauma 'processing' stage of the therapy. These techniques may include mindfulness, breathing exercises or Emotional Freedom Technique (EFT, see Chapter 4) (Craig, 2011). EFT calms the nervous system by tapping certain meridian points. This initial stage also includes giving the client information about the approach, normalising and validating symptoms, and ways to manage these symptoms.

Before embarking on any trauma therapy it is important to explore the resources and coping strategies clients have to support themselves throughout the treatment. One resource commonly used in EMDR is named a 'safe place'. The client will be asked to recall a pleasant memory, generally a memory where the client felt calm and content. They will be asked to bring the memory to the forefront of their minds by evoking the body sensations of sight, smell, taste, touch and sound. This enables the client to develop 'dual awareness' (Shapiro, 2006), so they can switch between the distressing memory and pleasant state memory, aiding the client to develop a sense of control over the trauma symptoms.

During the assessment session Chris described how he 'felt trapped'. He had been advised not to leave his hotel room until further notice. From his window he witnessed horrific scenes of violence on the streets below, magnified by the background noise of his TV blasting details of the event as it unfolded, including graphic images of a beheading on the Bosphorus Bridge. This constant exposure throughout the night, and the restriction of movement, created a 'freeze' response in Chris, as he felt 'helpless' and 'guilty' for not being able to do anything to help those being harmed on the streets below. Chris' aim for the six sessions was to reduce his trauma symptoms and build his resilience. He wanted to be confident about making an informed choice regarding whether to deploy to any future 'high risk' environments, rather than his 'fear' dictating that he could no longer go. As I asked Chris to complete a trauma assessment scale, the 'Impact of Events – Revised' questionnaire (Weiss, 2007), we explored his symptoms. He was having difficulty sleeping and regular panic attacks, and was experiencing intrusive thoughts and images about the event. He felt irritable and jumpy, and had difficulty with concentration and emotional outbursts. The fact that Chris had experienced these symptoms for over two months, and that his scores on the questionnaire were high, suggested that he was suffering from PTSD.

We concluded the assessment session by discussing Chris' treatment plan, and I explained how EMDR could help. We explored Chris' triggers, which included bangs, aeroplanes, helicopters and general loud noises. He was being triggered several times a day into a 'heightened state of arousal', where he would feel jumpy and on edge. The relaxation techniques developed during the stabilisation phase helped Chris calm his nervous system and manage his symptoms during and between sessions.

Session two

EMDR protocol

During the second session we set up the EMDR protocol. This involves identifying the worst moment of the traumatic event, naming the feelings associated with the moment, and identifying where the client experiences these feelings in their body.

When I ask clients where they notice a certain feeling in their body, they may look at me in a strange way. We tend to live in our heads most of the time but our bodies hold a wealth of information, with trauma energy becoming trapped on a cellular level and needing to be released for full recovery to take place. I have often heard clients describe a tingling sensation or electric pulse in a specific part of their body, as they are processing distressing memories. I encourage and reassure the client that this is a good sign and that their body is trying to release and process the incident. It always fascinates me where clients hold the emotional distress at a physical level. A female client who had been abused held a strong somatic sensation of a golf ball in her throat, and over a couple of sessions experienced the sensation of throwing it up, which enabled her to start to speak freely about her experiences. A male client's left shoulder ached intensely as we processed a memory of his wife leaving him. He imagined strapping it up throughout several of our sessions, his imagination allowed him to combine his physical discomfort with his emotional pain. He was then able to give himself permission to take the time needed in his psychological recovery and let go of his conditioning of 'just get on with it' as he visualised each week that his shoulder was improving. For further reading detailing research about trauma being held in the body see *The Body Keeps the Score* (Van Der Kolk, 2014) and *The Body Remembers* (Rothschild, 2017).

For Chris, the worst moment of the traumatic event was 'the sound of an explosion'. The feelings this provoked for him were of 'fear, sadness and guilt'. Chris was feeling 'trapped' and 'frozen' as he felt 'helpless'. I asked Chris where he experienced these feelings in his body. He had a body sense of 'tightness in his upper chest, and a churning feeling in his stomach'. We then explored what negative cognition Chris held about himself when recalling this distressing memory. In this instance, Chris held a negative belief of 'I am weak', with his preferred positive cognition being 'I am strong'. At this point of his therapy he could not believe this more constructive perspective.

We all hold some negative beliefs about ourselves, often developed from our childhood. When things are going well and we feel happy and resilient these negative beliefs remain dormant. However, when we are placed out of our comfort zone, feel pressurised or have experienced a traumatic incident, the negative self-beliefs become activated. They begin to make an excessive amount of noise in our heads and can often hold a great deal of power over us. These negative beliefs can include thoughts such as: I am weak, I am to blame, I am a bad person, I am worthless, I am damaged, I am not loveable, I am powerless. Often perfectionists hold a negative self-belief of 'I am a failure', resulting in high expectations of self and others. In EMDR these beliefs are divided into four categories: responsibility (I am defective), responsibility (I did something wrong), safety/vulnerability and control/choice (Shapiro, 2006).

Session three

Desensitisation/processing

As Chris had good resources, and was able to self-regulate through relaxation exercises, we were able to progress into the 'processing' stage. We used eye movements for the bilateral stimulation. This stage of the therapy is often client-led, as the client is asked to reflect on the incident and go with whatever comes up. As the BLS stimulates the client's natural processing the client starts to make a narrative of the events, and may stumble across the 'stuck moments' (the moments in time that caused some disturbance for the client and need further processing). Most of the time the therapist just states 'go with that', so as not to interrupt the natural healing process that is being activated. The therapist will be tracking the client in detail and at times may respond further depending on what is emerging.

CT: I feel anxious and scared, wanting to run away, run to safety.

T: Go with that.

CT: blurred in head, brain wanting to shut down. It feels heavy, it is too much. I feel sleepy.

(Chris had coped with the trauma by shutting down or going to sleep – his natural coping mechanism was being triggered. Often it takes time for the client to fully trust the process of EMDR and there can be some resistance in the initial stages.)

CT: I feel like I have to reassure myself all the time. I'm safe, it is going to be OK.

T: Go with that, just noticing, just observing.

CT: So scary, suddenly everything went quiet. All the mosques started chanting. That was so scary. I didn't understand. That moment plays on my mind. It didn't feel safe. Starting to make plans in my head, where is the exit route, what if someone comes into my room, what if my window gets blown off.

T: Go with that, you are doing well.

CT: The back of my neck and shoulders are so tense.

(Clients often describe strong body sensations as they begin to process the trauma. This can be quite unnerving for the client, but it is a sign that the trauma energy is shifting. Therefore it is helpful for the therapist to encourage the client and reassure them that they are doing well. If the distress becomes overwhelming we may carry out a relaxation technique.)

CT: Part of me wants to shut down. I feel numb.

CT: Part of me wants to move on, so angry.

T: If you gave the anger a voice what would it say?

(I often highlight the anger response and ask the client for an expression of the anger, as it starts to activate an empowering energy, rather than a frozen, helpless energy.)

CT: It scares me to feel angry. I'm scared of my own feelings of anger.

T: Go with that. If you let it out what would happen?

CT: I would hurt people.

CT: I feel numb. I feel lonely.

CT: Ball of fear exploded in my chest. In my head I have the words, I am letting people down. But then when I connect to my anger I heard the words, I am letting myself down. Whirlwind in my head.

(The client is swinging between the old coping mechanisms of wanting to shut down, feeling numb, and connecting to a new protective energy activated through his anger response, of not wanting to let himself down. The above statement shows a move from the freeze, to the flight, to the fight response. The fight response can enable a client to begin to feel more empowered.)

Session four

Self-compassion

CT: I feel sad for the people and soldiers on that bridge. The ugly side of humanity. I was watching images on TV of a man being beheaded on the bridge. I was scared a crowd of people could do that. The following night there were celebrations in the street. It was not a celebration. It felt aggressive, this was just as scary.

T: Go with that.

CT: How surreal an image of the garbage truck stuck in my head. The next day cleaning up the streets. People in restaurants. As if nothing had happened. I remember thinking the first night how beautiful everything was. Now it had lost all its beauty.

(The aftermath of a traumatic event can be just as disturbing as the event itself. A client's view of the world can be fundamentally changed. The surreal silence often following a trauma can feel very unnerving as the body will still be on heightened alert.)

CT: I feel guilty and weak for not helping those people.

T: Imagine it was a colleague of yours, what would you be saying to them?

CT: They did a good job under a difficult situation.

T: Try saying that to yourself.

CT: I find it hard. I feel stupid and a failure.

T: So you call yourself stupid and a failure when you are vulnerable.

(A common interweave is to ask the client what their perception of a close friend would be if they were in the same situation. We can be experts in berating ourselves and not offering ourselves the same support and comfort we would offer to a close friend. An interweave may move the processing on if blocked or introduce new adaptive information.)

CT: Huge wave of sadness. Anger at self, letting myself down (cries).

CT: I won't give up on myself.

CT: I came home and didn't ask for help. I forgot about myself. I want to take better care of myself.

(Chis is beginning to shift his cognitive belief of 'I am weak' and is beginning to feel more compassion towards himself.)

Session five

Changing self-belief

CT: Sad, sad for the soldiers, the country, the people we met, the refugees we had talked to, chaos, everything changes so fast. I feel it in my arms.

T: What do your arms need to do?

CT: (The client automatically clenches his fists.) Makes me feel strong (pushes arms out from chest). Strength is also active, I don't know how I can be strong in a non-active, non-fighting way. It requires a lot of effort from me.

(I often encourage clients to express the movement that seems to be trapped in their body. This expression helps to release the trauma energy. In Sensorimotor Therapy this would be carried out consciously and in slow motion. For example, many rape victims need to act out 'pushing the perpetrator away' in a safe and contained way within the therapy, especially if they couldn't at the time, due to being drugged or stuck in the freeze response.)

CT: Image of me screaming in anger.

T: Go with that.

CT: (There were noises of planes overhead during the session.) Leave me alone, shut up, just let me be. Leave me alone!

CT: I am so angry. The anger is out, it can't be put back now.

CT: Whirlwind in my head, dizzy.

(Chris was shouting at the planes passing overhead.)

CT: But I handled the situation well, I'm taking charge in resolving issues.

CT: I'm a freaking hero (laughs). Actually I do handle quite a lot. I actually held it together so well. I still managed to report back, write a report, carry out a good piece of work, and look after my colleagues. (Chris straightens his back and holds his arms firmly.)

(Chris was beginning to connect to his inner strength, cognitively, psychologically and physically.)

CT: It's going to be OK. I'm going to be OK. The way I feel is normal. I'm going to be OK eventually.

Each time Chris started a session he would report that his trauma symptoms were decreasing. Chris was becoming less triggered, experienced fewer intrusive thoughts and was able to concentrate better. He would use his 'safe place' exercise between sessions to reduce his anxiety.

Session six

Ending session

Chris had not been able to read or watch anything about the event since returning home. Between sessions five and six he decided to watch a YouTube video of the incident. (It is important to note here that the timing of this has to be right, as some individuals may feel re-traumatised from watching this material; obviously for Chris he felt ready and able to watch this video without being triggered.) When he returned for session six Chris said that by watching the video, 'It had put something to rest. It was a big deal. I had a right to freak out about it. I did handle things well.' Chris was no longer jumpy at loud noises or being triggered by aeroplanes: 'I can look up at a plane now and feel normal, my heart is no longer racing.' He was considering returning to Istanbul and felt 'clear-headed' to make choices about future deployments.

We carried out the installation stage of the EMDR therapy. This is where we install the positive cognition 'I am strong', holding in mind the distressing memory using the bilateral stimulation. Chris ended the therapy saying 'this is not in me anymore. There is some distance between the incident and me now'. I often hear clients describe a sense of distance between the traumatic event and the present day once therapy is complete. This demonstrates to me that the incident has been processed in the brain, moving the incident away from the amygdala (the regularly activated 'fire alarm' system) to the hippocampus (the 'filing system'). Chris can now choose when (or, indeed, if) he wants to think about the event, rather than the event holding control over him and 'reappearing' in the form of flash-backs and ruminating thoughts.

Following EMDR Chris completed the Impact of Events questionnaire which showed his trauma symptoms had significantly reduced. Six months after Chris' treatment he described how:

> I have recently gone through an intense security training exercise, using pyrotechnics to simulate gunshots, and simulating kidnapping. I was surprised that this did not trigger any symptoms, instead I felt calm. The treatment continues to be effective. I am now able to deploy to environments where the security and political situation is volatile.

TF-CBT: how does it work?

Cognitive Behavioural Therapy (CBT) was first developed in the 1960s. The approach is based on the theories of American psychiatrist Aaron T. Beck's work on Cognitive Therapy, combined with American psychologist Albert Ellis' work on Rational Emotive Behaviour Therapy (REBT) (Dobson & Block, 1988). CBT has been used to help people with depression, anxiety, stress, obsessive compulsive disorder (OCD), panic disorder, phobias, eating disorders, anger management and addictions. It is the most widely used evidence-based therapeutic approach and is the treatment of choice by the National Health Services (NHS) in the UK. Many NHS Trusts now implement CBT and/or EMDR to work with patients who are traumatised.

CBT focuses on building coping and problem-solving strategies. The focus is on the client's present state rather than on past events. CBT aims to identify the client's distorted thinking patterns, modify beliefs and change behaviours. CBT is made up of six phases:

1   assessment;
2   reconceptualisation;
3   skills acquisition;

4   skills consolidation and application training;
5   generalisation and maintenance;
6   post-treatment assessment follow-up (Gatchel & Rollings, 2008).

The third wave of CBT is moving towards incorporating mindfulness (Graham, 2014).

Trauma-Focused CBT (TF-CBT) was developed in the 1980s by Drs Anthony Mannarino (clinical psychologist), Judith Cohen (professor of psychiatry) and Esther Deblinger (clinical psychologist). The initial research was conducted with children and adolescents, but the approach also works well for adults (Ehlers et al., 2013). The therapeutic elements of TF-CBT are denoted by the 'PRACTICE' acronym: Psychoeducation; Relaxation; Affective expression & regulation; Cognitive coping; Trauma narrative development and processing; In vivo gradual exposure; Conjoint parent–child sessions (children only); Enhancing safety and future development (Cohen, 2006). TF-CBT therapy can include 'homework' between sessions.

The case study below incorporates several TF-CBT techniques.

Case study 2 (TF-CBT)

I was working in Nepal and just happened to be out there when the earthquake struck. I didn't know what to do, I was in shock. It all happened so quickly. It is not something you can prepare for. I was walking to work when the earth started to move. I dropped to the ground. When I picked myself up I was covered in dust. For some reason I decided to walk back towards my flat. When I got there, to my horror, I realised the building was no longer there. I had become close to the lady in the flat below me, who had a young daughter. Her daughter was ten and often played in the streets. She was shy but would smile up at me as I walked to work in the mornings, with her bouncy pigtails tied back with pink ribbons. All I could hear was her mother's gut-wrenching cries as she frantically looked for her daughter. I felt numb; was this really happening?

I noticed I had blood on my hands. Was it my blood? Was it someone else's blood? I thought no one would find me, no one would know where I was. We were all huddled together for the next few days as we were waiting to be evacuated home. But so many people had lost everything – their homes, their families and friends, their livelihoods. I remember holding back my tears, trying to help the family as much as I could before being notified that I was to be evacuated home. I was being pulled out as other aid workers were arriving to help with the aftermath.

(Annika, aid worker)

Sessions one/two

Assessment/resourcing/formulation

Annika came for six sessions of specialist trauma counselling, having been signed off sick. She was referred through her GP, who had diagnosed Annika as having PTSD. Her symptoms included difficulty sleeping, intrusive thoughts, low morale and energy, comfort eating and an increase in alcohol consumption, which was something for the therapist and client to monitor. It is not uncommon that some clients will self-medicate through alcohol or substances in the early stages of experiencing a trauma.

I carried out a thorough assessment session during which we identified Annika's triggers, which included people contacting her from work, sirens, similar incidents on the news or TV programmes, and being on trains (the movement reminded her of the earthquake, the ground feeling unstable). We practised mindfulness and breathing exercises in the initial sessions, which Annika used to support herself between sessions. Annika bought a journal to keep notes of her sessions, which can be a really helpful way for clients to keep track of their own progress. Annika described herself as 'a hardened aid worker', having worked in the field for over 12 years. She introduced herself as someone who had 'seen it all'. She had been deployed to Afghanistan, South Sudan and Bangladesh over the last year. She had been working in Nepal for six weeks when the earthquake hit. She said she was already feeling exhausted from her previous deployments, and needed a break. As we progressed through her assessment Annika shared that other distressing memories still 'haunt' her. Two particular memories seemed to cause a level of distress: a man improvising the act of masturbation in front of her whilst she was travelling through Juba; and the second, witnessing a suicide car bomb in Iraq. The thread that seemed to connect all of the distressing memories that were 'haunting' Annika was her distorted self-belief of 'I am worthless'. She imagined being trapped in the rubble and that no one would find her, she imagined being blown up by the car bomb or assaulted by the man making rude gestures towards her, and no one would come to her aid.

Annika had been brought up in a military family and her conditioning was 'to get on with it'. Her family had high expectations of her and respected intellect and success. The cumulative impact of this conditioning over the years was that Annika found it hard to show her feelings or reach out for support when she was struggling, or even recognise the signs that she might be struggling. She described herself as 'highly independent'. Her focus was to help others, but this had been to the detriment of looking after herself. Indeed it was actually a close friend of Annika's that said to her 'I think you should get some specialist help', having noticed a change in Annika's behaviour. She experienced Annika becoming more impatient, angry, depressed and generally not taking care of herself. Annika had good resources, including swimming, running, yoga, socialising and painting; however, at this time she was becoming more isolated and less motivated to do any exercise. At assessment Annika evidenced signs of suffering from compassion fatigue and burnout. She said that she wanted to stop her intrusive thoughts and be able to have a good night's sleep.

Session three

Trauma processing

We agreed to work through all three distressing memories, and Annika chose to work on the man stimulating masturbation first. She was in a vehicle with other local staff, all male. No one spoke of the incident, and Annika did not mention it at the time. But as she caught the eye of the perpetrator she felt a 'shiver go down my spine'. She could still feel this 'cold shockwave' down her back every time she brought the memory to mind. When a client mentions a strong somatic sensation activated from a distressing moment in time I sometimes work using a form of visualisation. This is often a gentle way of processing distressing memories, as it encourages the client to make contact with their body and work through any somatic emotional excess that has become an unwelcome resident in their body. Annika closed her eyes and brought her attention and breath to the discomfort in her body.

T: Take your focus and breathe into that sensation in your body of the 'cold shockwave'.
CT: It feels so cold, like ice is running through my veins.
T: Just notice that, as if an observer.
CT: (Annika shudders) Urgh it is so uncomfortable.
T: Does it have a size, colour, words, texture?
CT: It is like ice water running downwards along my spine. I feel goose bumps all over. No one noticed, or chose not to. Like it is the norm. I felt completely violated.
CT: No one cares, no one would protect me. I felt like I had to just put up with it and accept it. I wanted to scream at him, in his face, and say, how dare you, you are disgusting, but I couldn't. In that moment I felt frozen. Cold to the core.
CT: Urgh, no wonder I feel so cold in my body, it makes sense now.
T: What does that cold feeling need from you?

CT: I want to cuddle under the duvet with a hot water bottle. (Laughs) I remember having a girlie night in, and three of my friends and I just sat in our pyjamas, drank wine and cuddled up with hot water bottles.

Through the visualisation Annika felt supported, seen and protected by her friends. She added a hot water bottle into the sensation of ice running down her back and she described feeling her body 'thaw out'. The visualisation led Annika to process the memory to the point that it no longer had any impact on her; without the visualisation Annika would not have connected the feeling in her back with that particular incident. As demonstrated, guided visualisation opens the client's mind to finding creative solutions for their own recovery, which can enable distressing memories to be fully processed. I will encourage a client to give themselves permission to do whatever they need to through imagination, as it is important that they don't feel judged in any way as they are trying to make sense and process distressing memories.

Session four

Trauma processing

In this session we focused on processing the car bomb memory. The noise the bomb made as it exploded was the most disturbing part of the memory for Annika. It was at the point of explosion that she described feeling her 'bones shatter' and an overwhelming sense of fear. Noise, smell and taste can become the most disturbing parts of a memory. I suggested that Annika imagine that the sound was playing on a radio and she had the controls. I then asked if she could imagine turning the sound down. Over time she was able to reduce the sound and watch the memory in silence. She went one step further and changed the sound to a squeaky child's toy, one that her daughter had and always made her giggle. She imagined an ABBA tune blasting out of the radio of the car, which continued to play after the explosion. Using imagination to manipulate a memory can significantly reduce the level of distress. This can be done by adding humour, reducing the size of someone who you feel has power over you, or adding a silly voice to a challenging colleague or manager.

Sessions five and six

Trauma processing/ending

The final memory Annika wanted to work on was the earthquake. The worst moment of this memory was the pink ribbons poking out of some rubble, knowing the neighbour's daughter was buried below, combined with the sound of the mother's primal screams, and the blood she saw on the street.

Annika imagined the memory playing on a TV screen and she had the remote control. She would talk through the memory and pause it at the 'stuck moments'. As with the sound of the car bomb, we manipulated the image of the earthquake. Initially Annika was trying to turn the memory into a black and white movie. She managed to remove the colour except the red blood. The blood seemed to be growing and getting larger. Annika became tearful at this point. 'How am I supposed to let go of this memory of a little girl dying?' she asked. 'She had such a sweet smile. It would be disrespectful to try to blank her out.' Clients who have lost a loved one often find it hard to process a traumatic bereavement, as they feel the process may interfere with their memories of the person they hold so dear to their heart. There is a resistance of letting go, and a deep longing to hold on. I reassure the client that by processing the trauma it does not mean they are losing memories of their loved one. The grieving process will take longer than the trauma processing, but often the client needs to heal from the trauma first so the grieving process can begin.

As we worked through this memory Annika did begin to feel a deep sense of loss for the young girl, which she hadn't connected with before. Eventually the red began to fade into a paler pink colour, which Annika then connected to the colour of the young girl's hair ribbons. Often when the trauma is processed and grieving starts, I ask the client if there is anything they feel they need to do symbolically to lay the person to rest respectfully. In this instance, two months after the therapy had finished, Annika returned to Nepal and laid some pink flowers at the place where her young smiley neighbour had died.

By the end of the sessions Annika had returned to work on a gradual return plan, her energy had increased and she was no longer suffering from burnout. Annika has not had any trauma symptoms since the therapy and is able to deploy to high-risk environments again.

I will never forget the things I witnessed. They will always be part of me, but they no longer hold any control over me. When I think about them they seem in the past and no longer impact me in a negative way. As with any troubling event we always learn and take something from it. The treatment I received allowed me to do that, and rather than just blocking it out and trying to forget about it, I've been able to move forward and am stronger for it.

4   Resilience toolkit

The first aid kit

Due to a great deal of research in neuroscience, the understanding of trauma has advanced over the last two decades. This knowledge has brought a wealth of insight into how to manage acute stress and trauma symptoms. The good news is that there are many techniques that individuals can use to build their resilience. The previous two chapters have explored how trauma affects the brain and body. I will now look at techniques that can counteract these effects, and can subsequently reduce traumatic and acute stress. In this chapter I endeavour to describe and explain what resilience techniques make up the 'first aid kit' of trauma care. These techniques are a combination of eastern and western resources, and are used globally. 'We can directly train our arousal system by the way we breathe, chant, and move, a principle that has been utilised since time immemorial in places like China and India, and in every religious practice' (Van Der Kolk, 2014, p. 207).

Building resilience is about learning to respect and take care of yourself, I have created a resilience toolkit acronym using the word RESPECT. I recommend accumulating a good balance of resources that cover the following areas: Relaxation, Education, Social, Physical, Exercise, Creativity and Thinking.

- Relaxation: *finding a way to calm and relax the body.*
- Education: *understanding the mechanics of trauma.*
- Social: *making and keeping supportive social connections.*
- Physical: *coming into contact with our physical body.*
- Exercise: *staying active.*
- Creativity: *activating the creative part of the brain.*
- Thinking: *challenging the negative thinking that can consume the mind after a trauma.*

I suggest you try out some of the techniques below in order to create your own personal resilience toolkit, to help yourself and others when needed.

Relaxation

Calming the system when we are traumatised or feel acute stress is essential, and the first step in stabilisation. I explained in Chapter 2 how the autonomic nervous system is activated into the survival response, creating anxiety and nervous energy. Through relaxation techniques we can teach the body to regulate back into a calm state. If you are new to meditation it may be useful to start with guided meditations to enable the mind to have something to focus on, rather than sitting in silent meditations, where you may become consumed with 'negative' thoughts.

- Breathing exercise:

> Balanced breathing is thought to have many benefits; such as helping nutrients be absorbed, boosting the immune system, contributing to bone growth, increasing circulation, strengthening organ functions, and even relieving pain. Relaxed, balanced breathing has even been shown to sometimes help panic attacks and migraines or to lessen the symptoms of asthma. With every deep breath, internal organs are massaged, circulation is enhanced, and lymph flow is increased. In short good breathing promotes good health.
>
> (Ogden & Fisher, 2015)

A simple breathing exercise I encourage clients to try is to take a deep breath in, hold for a couple of seconds and make the 'out breath' longer than the 'in breath'. This activates the parasympathetic nervous system, avoids hyperventilation, and allows our mind and body to relax. Therefore find you own comfortable count for the in breath and the out breath, making the out breath longer.

- Mindfulness: research shows that mindfulness helps to stabilise our moods, improve sleep, reduce anxiety, deepen concentration and improve self-compassion (Brown, Ryan & Creswell, 2007). Mindfulness enables us to 'listen' to our body. The body holds a wealth of information, and to stay healthy it is vital that we learn how to listen to the signs from our body that inform us of our stress levels and discomfort, before our body eventually forces us to stop through illness. Kabat-Zinn, world-renowned mindfulness teacher, describes mindfulness as 'Paying attention in a particular way; on purpose, in the present moment and nonjudgmentally' (Kabat-Zinn, 2005). Research on the benefits of mindfulness in the workplace demonstrated increased job performance, job satisfaction, improved work–life balance, and enhanced focus and concentration (Rebb & Atkins, 2015).

- I usually start with a simple exercise asking the client to focus on their breathing; breathing in the word 'calm', and breathing out the word 'tension'. When the client becomes comfortable doing this I may add a colour to the in and out breath, for example breathing in 'calm' with a blue or green colour, and breathing out 'tension' with a red or black colour.

Yasmin is an aid worker, living and working in Lebanon. Reflecting on how chaotic her life has been in recent years, she says: 'I've been rushing from one thing to another. I feel like I haven't breathed properly for a long time.' After a great deal of resistance, she finally started using breathing and mindfulness exercises. She no longer suffers from acute stress, and uses her practices daily whilst at work.

- Aid workers can take on a great deal of responsibility, often more than their role requires. Therefore I recommend the 'letting go' exercise. I ask the client to imagine a magnet floating at arm's length in front of their torso. I then suggest they breathe in the word 'relaxation' and breathe out the word 'letting go'. As they do this I ask them to imagine releasing all the responsibilities that are not theirs, onto the magnet floating in front of them. At the end of the exercise I ask them to imagine the magnet floating to, and dissolving into, the ground below.
- There are many free mindfulness downloads you can access on the internet.

- Anchors: anchors are items that ground us. These can be photographs of loved ones or of a beautiful place we have visited, a pebble from a beach, an item of jewellery, an item that symbolises our faith, a crystal, etc. Generally the best anchors are small so that we can carry them with us. When we look at this anchor it manifests a positive mood, happy thoughts, and can assist us in staying grounded.
- Grounding: another way to stay grounded is to stand tall: drop your shoulders and back down, pull your stomach in, and push your chest out, as if standing against a wall. Imagine a thread pulling from the top of your head to the ceiling, stretching out your spine. Now imagine your body is as strong as a tree trunk, with roots growing out through your feet and into the ground below. When we focus on our feet rooted firmly to the floor, we move our focus from the noise in our head to a solid and calm place in our body, and start to connect with the present moment rather than the distressing memory. If you are supporting someone who may have just experienced a flashback, or is

acutely distressed, you can help them with grounding through asking what he/she notices in the immediate surroundings. Address them using their name regularly, and ask them the time and date, including the year. All these things will help ground the individual and enable them to focus on the here and now, rather than the trauma memory.

- Prayer: neurotheology considers brain functions from a spiritual perspective. 'The more you focus on something ... the more that becomes your reality, the more it becomes written into the neural connections of your brain' (Newberg & Waldman, 2009). This philosophy is similar to Hebbian theory that 'neurons that fire together, wire together' (Hebb, 1949). Newberg found that when studying individuals, of various faiths, during prayer, their frontal lobes lit up (linked to positive mood), but the parietal lobes (linked to sense of self) went dark. Individuals described this 'as a sense of oneness with the universe'. Further research suggests that meditation and prayer can tame the amygdala (the fire alarm) by reducing anxiety and, by feeling connected to the universe, form a greater acceptance of self and others.
- Sleep: sleep is often the first thing to deteriorate when we are stressed or traumatised. All the techniques described in this trauma toolkit will help to improve sleep quality.

Jacob, a doctor, was deployed to Malawi:

All I could see when I closed my eyes at night was the desperation in the woman's eyes as she held her baby. I knew then that the baby was not going to make it. I felt so helpless, and responsible in some way. This went on for several weeks. I just couldn't sleep. I kept thinking of my own children.

Simon's first deployment was to South Sudan: 'I probably didn't sleep for the first month. It just took me so long to adapt to my environment, witnessing so much torture and hardship.'

- Creating a routine at bedtime is helpful. This can include having a shower or bath, or if we are anxious about workload it may be helpful to write a 'to do' list before going to bed, reassured that we can come back to the information when we wake in the morning and don't have to hold it in our minds throughout the night. If we are haunted by trauma memories, imagine placing them in a box, and watching the box float away into the distance.

- If we are struggling to sleep our brain can become agitated, releasing hormones that make us more and more anxious. Therefore, we need to be mindful of our self-talk when we are lying in bed. I went through a phase of struggling to sleep and I would say to myself, 'I am comfortable and I am safe', which enabled me to stay in a more relaxed state. This is clearly not possible in certain contexts, but the point here is to observe the self-talk and change the negative statement to something more positive, for example, 'I'm going to have a terrible day tomorrow if I don't get to sleep' versus 'my body is relaxing, even if I am not asleep'.
- Turn off 'blue light' technology, ideally one hour before going to sleep: TV, laptops, mobile phones, iPads, etc.
- Manage your circadian rhythms by avoiding bright light in the evening, and expose yourself to sunlight in the morning.
- Breathing exercises, yoga stretches, mindfulness and prayer can all help to induce a relaxed state before going to sleep.
- A hot glass of milk draws the blood supply to the gut, and creates a slight fall to the supply in the brain, producing drowsiness. Camomile tea is known for its relaxing qualities.
- Placing drops of lavender, camomile, bergamot, jasmine, rose or sandalwood oil on the pillow, wrists or bath, or burning oils in an oil burner, can help promote good quality sleep.
- Autogenic exercises respond to verbal instruction, which then enables the body to relax and helps to control breathing, blood pressure, heartbeat and body temperature (Manzoni, Pagnini, Castelnuovo & Molinari, 2008). This can result in a deep relaxation, and in turn reduce stress. Repeat these instructions to the body three times: 'my left arm is warm and heavy'. Then focus on your 'right arm', 'left leg', 'right leg', 'neck and shoulders'. Then end the exercise with the statement 'my breathing is calm and regular', again repeated three times.

Education

Stabilisation is the initial stage of good trauma therapy. This consists of psycho-education, normalisation and building resources. Understanding the trauma response, trauma symptoms, and how to support someone who is traumatised or acutely stressed, will help to normalise the impact of trauma. Within this context, I often refer to the statement 'Facts Fight

Fear'. Focusing on facts in the initial stages enables the prefrontal cortex part of the brain to stay online, thus reducing anxiety levels.

- Psycho-education: trauma symptoms are often described as *a normal reaction to an abnormal event.* Understanding how our physiology is impacted by trauma and acute stress helps to normalise symptoms, and reassure an individual who is suffering. Chapter 2 explains the basics of trauma awareness, and anyone deploying to a high-risk environment should know this information to support themselves, colleagues, local partners or beneficiaries. It is also important that the individual has some techniques (such as those listed in this chapter) in their resilience toolkit to assist themselves, or others, in distress. Try gathering some techniques from this chapter and Chapter 2, to build your confidence in supporting colleagues. Start by considering how might you support the aid worker, below, who had just been raped.

> The next hours find me scrubbing my body in the shower, trying to erase an invisible layer that will take more than a year to fully slough off.... My post-sexual assault training had flown from my mind. The one friend I've told everything to reminds me that I need to get tested for HIV and STIs, that I need to take the morning after pill and post-exposure prophylactics (PEP). On the Monday morning I travel to the MSF clinic, in a daze. It feels like I am watching my body from above somehow – both present and not present.
>
> (Megan Nobert, founder of Report the Abuse, shares her story in Chapter 5)

- Triggers: the amygdala stores the visual images of trauma as sensory fragments from our five senses. If the information is not processed to the hippocampus (the filing system), then one of the senses could become triggered, by a visual image, a smell, sound, taste or touch. This activates the survival response, which results in the individual feeling 'as if' they are back in the trauma memory. Anniversaries, birthdays and other significant dates can also become triggers.

Mark, a senior security coordinator who spent five years deploying to war-torn countries, explained: 'every time I hear a loud bang, or a plane overhead, I jump. I feel on edge, I feel physically sick.' Tim, a logistics manager, arrived for his trauma counselling in a panic, clearly having just experienced a flashback. 'I don't know what happened – it just came out of the blue. It started at the gas station around the corner, as I was filling up my car with petrol.' As we explored this further it became apparent that the smell of petrol had triggered his flashback of an explosion in Juba, where one of his colleagues had died.

- Dual awareness: dual awareness is a technique where an individual holds awareness of one or more experiences, simultaneously. When experiencing traumatic stress an individual can become consumed with the 'internal' experience of the traumatic event, and lose connection with all other 'external' experiencing. Therefore it is useful to practice experiencing multiple events simultaneously, as we do in normal everyday life. Think of an event that causes some distress, say level 5 out of 10 (therefore not an overwhelming level of distress), and notice what sensations you feel in your body and your emotional state. Then divert your attention to your environment. Name one thing you hadn't noticed about your environment before. Ask yourself questions, such as what colours do I notice? What smells do I notice? What sensations do I have on my skin? What is the temperature? Now divert your attention back and forth between the two experiences, and notice the changes in your body and mood each time you do so. This helps to develop dual awareness. Van Der Kolk describes an 'experiencing self' and an 'observer self' (Van Der Kolk, 2014). The 'experiencing self' is 'experiencing the distressing memory', while the 'observing self' is aware of the immediate environment, and grounded in the present moment. Dual awareness becomes 'a tool for braking and containment' (Rothschild, 2000, p. 129).

Social

Trauma is often related to attachment theory. Attachment is the emotional bond formed between people, in order to establish a sense of security and safety. Although attachment begins in infancy, the need for attachment relationships continues throughout our life. Trauma experiences can undermine attachments, and cause alienation. Therefore it is important to stay connected and maintain social engagement, as many individuals may want to isolate themselves. We often hear in the media about the distressing voicemail messages left on loved ones' phones as a major trauma is occurring; the 7/7 bombings (UK, 2005), the 9/11 terrorist attack (United States, 2001) and the Indian Ocean tsunami (Asia, 2004). Individuals want to reach out to their families, cry out for help, or in fatal incidents say their goodbyes. Social support networks, such as family, friends, colleagues, community or religious figures, can be at the crux of our recovery.

- Social connections: research into resilience is undisputed on the value of contact with loved ones as a supportive factor, and involving social networks in the healing process is thought to be very important (Jeanette & Scoboria, 2008). So, keeping in contact with close family and friends is a helpful resource. Many aid workers begin to feel 'a burden' and that 'no one understands' due to the nature of their work. Therefore, even if support is available, the difficulty many have is reaching out and asking for it. Additionally, when talking to someone about distressing experiences, monitor how it makes you feel. Do you come away feeling held, heard and supported, or do you feel more anxious and re-traumatised? Consider and monitor whom you talk to, and when or whether it helps or not.
- Socialising: aid workers can often feel 'guilty' for having fun and experiencing pleasure when they have been exposed to traumatic experiences on deployment. Give yourself permission to have fun again. Try not to isolate yourself; balance out alone time with socialising time.
- Team building: in my experiences of having supported so many staff teams after a traumatic event, I notice the deep connection between individuals who have 'been in this together'. This is recognised as 'trauma bonding', and in this way, colleagues can become a great source of support for one another.

David Kinchin, in his book *Post Traumatic Stress Disorder* (2001), describes this phenomenon when he writes about the Dunblane School massacre, where 16 children and a teacher were shot in Scotland, and the Aberfan disaster in Wales, where a waste tip from a Welsh coal field slid down the side of a valley, killing 116 children and 28 adults. 'This tragic shooting provided the largest incident of "trauma bonding"', he writes.

> In particular, there developed a bond between the residents of Dunblane and those living in Aberfan. The two disasters were separated by thirty years and about 315 miles of countryside, but the two communities were united in an invisible 'trauma bond'. This bond is an invisible understanding which exists between those who have witnessed or experienced a traumatic event.
>
> (Kinchin, 2001, p. 4)

Teams have been creative in their recovery and team building after a traumatic event, for example by setting up a table tennis room or a chill out room, or organising social events to informally build team spirit. 'Activity as simple as trying to keep a beach ball in the air as long as possible helps groups become more focused, cohesive, and fun', writes Van Der Kolk (2014, p. 355). On the flip side of this, if a group is not supported well after a traumatic event, 'splitting' can occur. I joined a large organisation soon after a mass scale traumatic event and witnessed a team that had become spilt. Half the team wanted to attend the frontline and offer workshops to support staff, half the team did not want to be on the frontline and stayed in the office taking calls and working individually with staff. Both these responses complemented each other in offering a comprehensive support programme, but animosity developed between the two different groups. This is an example of 'trauma splitting'. Individuals did not get good supervision, were not monitored in the level of involvement in the event, and there was no one to explain the impact of trauma on the team and organisation. The team became dysfunctional, leading to severe problems in communication and functioning, which became detrimental to staff wellbeing, resulting in grievances and scapegoating.

- Humour: humour is such an important resource after acute stress or trauma. Many of the organisations I have worked in, including Transport for London, the London Fire Brigade and the Metropolitan Police Service, have a culture of 'black humour'. It builds a sense of comradeship and connectedness. Out of context, or on the outside listening in, this may seem inappropriate, but I believe it is an important coping mechanism in building comradeship, and should not be frowned upon. It enables emergency personnel to 'vent their feelings, eliciting social support through the development of group cohesion, and distracting themselves from a situation, ensuring that they can act effectively' (Rowe, 2010).

Hamid, an aid worker, after a night of 'near miss' rocket and mortar attacks, stated that 'it was so surreal laughing over breakfast the next day, but such a good release and way of coping'.

- Peer support: creating a safe space where colleagues can talk openly about daily challenges and fears is known to promote a sense of psychological safety and reduce stress levels, which in turn bolsters engagement, learning and effectiveness.

Abdul was driving three doctors to a hospital in Kabul when the vehicle in front drove over an improvised explosive device (IED). He witnessed his colleague suffer severe injuries and tried to help in any way he could. Back in the compound he shared:

we all keep a close eye on each other. If someone seems 'zoned out' we check in with them and give them space to talk if they need to. You don't feel alone and there is no authoritative pressure, as your colleagues have been through the same thing and they understand, they do not judge you.

- Rituals and ceremonies: culturally prescribed political or religious rituals, ceremonies and/or healers can be a source of support. Culturally appropriate rituals enabled Mozambican refugees in Malawi to build resilience (Englund, 1998). There are so many varied ceremonies and rituals when we lose a loved one, depending on religious belief and culture. Often if a group of colleagues have lost one of the team they will set up a condolence book, lay flowers in a special place, or create a meaningful ritual in memory of the individual who has passed. After the Grenfell Tower fire (UK, 2017) where approximately 71 people died, the community came out in force and created a tribute wall so they could leave personal messages and prayers for those affected by the fire.
- Faith/religion: our spiritual beliefs, whether it is in relationship with Allah, Buddha, God or any other form of deity or spiritual guide, can bring comfort during distressing times. However, at the same time others can start to question or challenge their faith following a traumatic incident, for example asking why 'God' is allowing these terrible things to happen. 'Spirituality has been shown to have a significant impact on resilience in improving recovery rates in patients' (Tehrani, 2010).
- Pets/animals: many people get a great deal of comfort from their pets, or from animals in general. There are also many trauma therapy centres that use animals to encourage healing. The most prevalent outcomes were a reduction in depression, PTSD symptoms and anxiety. Several recovery centres use dogs or horses to help reduce symptoms of trauma and acute stress.

Physical

So much is written about trauma being held in the body. Through physical movement and learning to be in contact with our physical being, we can release some of the trauma energy.

- Shaking it off: when we feel tense it can help to literally 'shake it off', through shaking our hands vigorously, or waving our arms around each side of our body.

- Emotional Freedom Technique (EFT): EFT (Craig, 2011) comprises of tapping median points on our body, which is believed to release energy blockages from negative emotions. A simple version of this is to tap your collarbone several times and combine it with a statement such as, 'even though I am anxious, I am OK'. One series of tapping might include: top of the head, inner edge of one eyebrow, outer edge of same eyebrow, under the eye, above the lip, on the chin and down to the collarbone. Repeat the statement three times as you tap each area. The statement can be changed depending on the feeling: 'even though I am sad/depressed/lonely/angry etc., I am OK'. EFT has also been used to manage physical pain.
- Massage: when we are suffering acute stress or trauma, blood is pumped to the large muscles. Therefore any form of massage is helpful to encourage our muscles to relax. If you have the opportunity to go to a spa or a retreat this is an excellent way to recharge energy and build resilience. Also, doing this reinforces the message that we are worthy of self-care.
- Smell: smell is the quickest way to get information to the brain from all our senses. Therefore, when someone is triggered into a trauma memory, having a small bottle of scent at hand can be really grounding. Pick a smell that helps you, and try it out. I have lavender, rose, lemongrass, orange and peppermint in my therapy room.
- Health practitioners: visiting health practitioners such as chiropractors, naturopaths, herbalists, osteopaths or reflexologists may be beneficial, but do make sure they have a good understanding of acute stress and trauma.
- Diet: when we are experiencing acute stress the stomach shuts down, so it is helpful to routinely eat meals. If someone is experiencing nausea I would encourage them to eat little but often, so as to keep their stomach and digestive system activated. When our digestive system shuts down we experience a dry mouth, as we don't need to produce saliva to help digest our food. Therefore drinking lots of water is helpful. If you don't have water nearby, thinking about eating a lemon can cause the production of saliva. Try it! I recall someone placing a drop of lemon juice on their tongue each time they became triggered, which stabilised them immediately. *Alcohol, caffeine* and *nicotine* will keep the stress response activated.
- Nature: research has shown that even brief interactions with nature can promote improved cognitive functioning and overall wellbeing. Freedom from Torture, based in the UK, was set up to help survivors of torture, the majority of whom arrive in the UK as asylum seekers and refugees. Due to the diverse range of clients, it offers holistic

treatments, including reflexology, art therapy, physiotherapy and music therapy, and it also holds a drop-in chess club and gardening projects. The gardening projects enable a healing free open space where clients are encouraged to plant seeds, and nurture and watch these plants grow, comparable to creating new growth and a hope for the future.

Exercise

The stress response releases hormones such as adrenaline, nor-adrenaline and cortisol. When we exercise we release feel-good hormones, such as serotonin and endorphins.

- Exercise: being active not only helps us to keep fit, but research has shown that it also helps keep our minds alert. Exercise, in the form of walking, running, swimming, gym, cycling, etc., can help us to release the anxiety-provoking hormones from our body, and create feel-good hormones to replace them.
- Yoga, tai chi, qi gong and martial arts: these forms of exercise have been described as enhancing a spiritual or universal connection. The movements are performed in relationship with the breath, which encourages emotional regulation, with research also showing a reduction in heart rate variations (HRV). This enables control over our impulses and emotions, reduces anxiety and depression, and also the risk of physical illness (Sack, Hopper & Lamprecht, 2004). Van Der Kolk and colleagues evidenced how ten weeks of yoga markedly reduced PTSD symptoms (Van Der Kolk et al., 2014). These exercises not only calm our body, but also our minds.
- Building physical strength: building physical strength by exercising with weights has been shown to increase confidence. However, due to its adrenaline-pumping nature this type of exercise can become addictive; so if this technique is your preferred resource, make sure you balance it with resources from the other categories. Depending on the type of trauma incident, self-defence classes may be supportive of recovery. Such classes have been shown to support recovery for individuals who may have experienced sexual violence, for example. Core strength exercises such as Pilates can also encourage inner confidence and strength.

Creativity

We perceive trauma through sensory information. Creativity can soothe the traumatised parts of the brain, creating distraction as well as healing qualities.

- Art: painting or drawing is a great way to activate the creative part of the brain. This type of resource involves maintaining focus, and is therefore a good distraction that keeps us grounded in the present. Trauma can eliminate words, which art therapy can counteract as a creative outlet for self-expression. Art therapy is particularly effective with children and has often been used as a treatment for children in war zones, and survivors of torture. Dr Odelya Gertel Kraybill, developer of Expressive Trauma Integration (ETI), works with aid and development workers worldwide. She has successfully offered culturally sensitive approaches of expressive arts therapy with trauma survivors in South Africa, the Philippines, South Korea, China and Japan. The Tree of Life therapy, founded by Ncazelo Ncube and David Denborough (Denborough, 2008) and used worldwide, involves clients drawing a tree as a metaphor to represent different aspects of their lives.
- Music: music has often been used as a healer, connecting deeply to our emotions and offering comfort. Notice the music you are drawn to, and why. If you are listening to adrenaline-pumping music and you feel hyper-alert and anxious, you may want to listen to calming music for a while. It is helpful to recognise that for some individuals, certain songs can also be linked to a trauma memory and therefore become a trigger.

> I was working in Mozambique and was assaulted, resulting in being stabbed in the left shoulder. Around this time I was constantly listening to my favourite band. Now every time they are playing on the radio I have to turn it off. It takes me right back to that day.
>
> (Zara, Nairobi)

Music connects people, whether through attending events such as concerts, singing in a choir, or participating in various singing groups. These can all promote a sense of community, collaboration and focus. Cultures all over the world use drumming and dancing to process traumatic experiences. Bruce Perry explored the healing power of rhythm at the 2002 EMDR International Association Conference, relating this to the healing power of the bilateral stimulation method used in EMDR therapy, where he postulated that the calming effect rhythm has on us is hard-wired into the human nervous system. Indeed, music and dance were evidenced as effective trauma recovery techniques in African adolescent torture survivors (Harris, 2007). Rhythmic drumming also helped soldiers suffering PTSD, 'spontaneous drumming as a way to facilitate a sense of belonging, intimacy, togetherness, and connectedness; to achieve a non-intimidating access to traumatic memories; to allow an outlet for rage; and to regain a sense of control' (Bensimon, Amir & Wolf, 2008). Meanwhile, chanting is practised by many people around the world in searching for enlightenment, a connection to the divine, and a sense of wellbeing. Chanting connects the breath, mind, body and emotions through creating a healing vibration.

- Distraction: any creative activity that can be used as a distraction from trauma memories is helpful, particularly all-absorbing activities that keep the mind focused, such as sewing, puzzles, computer games, crafts, cooking, sculpture, etc.
- Writing: it can be helpful to just allow words to form on paper, with no judgement or pressure to 'get it right', but just using writing as a means to 'get it out there'. If it is an exercise in getting the 'bad stuff' out we may want to burn or destroy the written piece afterwards. Some people find journaling or keeping a diary of their experiences supportive. There are therapies that specifically focus on the healing power of the written word, such as Narrative Exposure Therapy (NET). NET has been field-tested in post-war societies such as Kosovo, Sri Lanka, Uganda and Somalia (Schauer, Neuner & Elbert, 2005). NET focuses predominantly on the client writing a detailed narrative timeline of all the traumatic events experienced.
- Balloons: I have asked clients to blow up balloons in therapy sessions. I love working creatively and if something may be helpful, then why not try it out? Blowing up balloons is extremely helpful for releasing feelings of 'rage' in a safe and contained way. The client might pop the balloon, bash it around the room a few times, or watch it fly away. I got this idea from watching a TED talk:

> In 2015 Cat Carter, an aid worker, gave a TED talk sharing some of her experiences (see Chapter 7). She tells a story of Nada, a five-year-old girl in Gaza, who witnessed the death of her family members during a bombing raid. Just beforehand her parents had asked Nada and her siblings to sing at the top of their voices to drown out the noises of the bombs. Nada became mute from this day onwards. The counsellor would say, 'think of everything that

is upsetting you today, all of that hurt, and that grief and that fear, and blow it into the balloon'. Even though Nada couldn't speak, the balloon therapy acknowledged Nada's feelings and gave her back a sense of control.

- Safe place: another exercise you can do to help relax your body and reassure yourself that you are safe is to do the 'safe place' exercise. This was originally used in hypnosis for reducing traumatic stress (Napier, 1996). Imagine a time when you were totally relaxed and happy. Make this memory one where you are still and on your own. Become aware of all your senses as you recall this event: what did you see, feel, hear, taste, touch and smell? How did you feel at the time and where do you notice that feeling in your body? Using sensory information, you can bring the memory alive, and recall it as a calming resource to use when you start to feel anxious.

Thinking

Our neurobiology changes after acute stress and trauma. The emotional brain, rather than the rational brain, dominates the mind. Therefore we can be consumed with thoughts of 'not being good enough', 'not having done enough', or feeling 'we are to blame'. These thoughts might 'feel' true, but they are often not based on reality.

- Challenging negative thoughts: as these negative thoughts can become all-consuming, it is important to challenge them. Consider what might you say to a friend who had experienced a similar event. Write down these supportive statements, and try saying them to yourself. In one session I suggested a client taped her voice on her mobile phone, stating something encouraging or positive such as 'I did everything I could under the circumstances'.
- Affirmations/mantras: write a couple of affirmations (supportive statements about yourself) and keep them nearby, to refer to regularly. Here are some examples clients have used to support themselves: 'I will look after myself', 'I am of value', 'I forgive those who have harmed me and I detach from them', 'I am a survivor and I am strong', 'I breathe in compassion', 'I free myself from fear and doubt'.
- Avoid big decisions: don't rush into making major life decisions directly after a traumatic event. A large humanitarian organisation noticed that a sizeable number of staff instigated relationship breakups after returning from the Ebola response deployments.

- Avoid stimuli: material on social media or TV can be triggering. Monitor what you are watching and your arousal levels. It may be that you need to spend a period of time avoiding certain subjects.
- Gradual exposure: if you find that you are avoiding a place, event or situation that reminds you of the trauma, write a ten-step plan of gradual exposure. For example, someone I worked with who had experienced a road traffic accident developed ten steps which included opening the car door, sitting in the driver seat, turning on the ignition, driving down the road and back, and gradually building up to driving to the place the accident happened. This all happened over a period of four weeks. It is important that these steps are small and manageable. Rate your anxiety level out of 10 (10 being the most anxious) for each step, as you are about to do it. If the next step rates over 5, add another step to reduce the anxiety level to 5 or below before continuing.

If trauma or acute stress symptoms persist for more than four weeks, in addition to practising some of the above techniques, it may be beneficial to seek out a trauma specialist therapy. There seems to be a great deal of confusion around what is best practice in trauma care and the timescales of delivery. The next chapter aims to demystify the various stages of managing critical incidents, and offers recommendations and clear guidelines for effective psychosocial support.

5   Psychosocial management of critical incidents

The emergency route

In responding to crises or emergencies of any kind, it is important to attend to the emotional and physical needs of those involved (Pardess, 2005; Sphere Project, 2004; IASC, 2017). A critical incident plan is the emergency route an organisation takes to support and minimise risk to staff, and enable effective and timely crisis management. Due to the nature of humanitarian aid work, critical incidents are an occupational hazard. A security policy does not replace a critical incident plan; both are needed and should be referred to in an emergency. A critical incident plan needs to include a 'trauma management programme', emphasising what psychosocial support is necessary to support staff through a major incident.

This chapter will focus on developing the 'trauma management programme' part of a critical incident plan. The trauma management programme should define every stage of a critical incident, from early intervention, trauma-specific treatments, follow-up, right through to recovery. A well thought-through critical incident plan saves lives and helps people recover quicker. Staff need training, guidance, knowledge and clear policies. The reality is that major incidents almost always catch us unaware; therefore, forward planning is essential.

As the lead on InterHealth Worldwide's Responding in a Crisis (RIC) service between April 2014 and April 2017, I gathered a significant amount of crisis response data (Dunkley, 2017). During that time, Inter-Health managed 188 critical incidents for 89 client organisations. The prevalence of each type of incident is shown in percentages, and the findings are below:

- Ill mental health (21 per cent). This refers to an individual suffering from the severe end of the spectrum of ill mental health, such as psychotic episodes or suicidal attempts or ideation.
- Civil unrest and terrorism (16 per cent). The data shows that civil unrest and terrorism has increased by 37 per cent over the last two

years. Many more countries have become targets of terrorist attacks over the last few years.

- Sexual violence (9 per cent). The data records that sexual violent crime has increased by 25 per cent over the last two years.
- Death of a member of staff due to accident/illness or murder (8.5 per cent).
- Kidnapping and hostage-taking (5 per cent), with an increase of 33 per cent over the last three years.
- Other incidents recorded: robbery, mugging, assault, vehicle accidents, carjacking, natural disasters, accidents and illnesses (non-fatal) and disease epidemic.

Due to the increase in risk to aid workers, many organisations have implemented in-house security teams or partnered with external security firms. However, while a great deal of attention is placed on a security risk assessment concerning the context and location of the deployment, what is often overlooked is the risk assessment of the profile of the individual being deployed. Jones, Denman and Molloy (University of East London) carried out a survey, 'Managing the security of aid workers with diverse profiles', looking specifically at assessing risk in relation to aid workers' diverse profiles regarding sexuality. The survey highlighted that 'diverse profiles were under-addressed in all security risk management processes' (Jones, Denman & Molloy, 2017). Lisa Reilly, Executive Director of European Interagency Security Forum (EISF) informed me that 'we need to meet legal responsibilities for non-discrimination and, at the same time, ensure individuals are informed about the additional risk due to their diverse profiles, i.e. nationality, ethnicity, age, gender, sexuality, and disability'. I saw a young woman who was suffering vicarious trauma after witnessing and experiencing many incidents of sexual harassment. She had been deployed to Congo early on in her career. She described being the only female member of staff working alongside a group of local male colleagues. She felt that she was 'not experienced enough', but 'did not want to let the organisation down, knowing how they had no one else to send'. It would have served well for the organisation to have carried out a risk assessment to determine the most appropriate individual to deploy, while considering what factors might need to be put in place to protect the member of staff.

In highlighting some of the items to consider in the stages of a trauma management programme I will explore two high-profile cases. Both Peter Moore, who was held hostage for just under three years in Iraq, and Megan Nobert, who was raped whilst working in South Sudan, agreed to speak to me in detail about their experiences. They both hope that some of the learning points that came out of their own horrific experiences will be taken forward and implemented into organisations' critical incident policies.

Peter Moore: case study

Iraqi militia held Peter Moore hostage for two years, seven months and one day. He was working in the 'Red Zone' in Bagdad, and living in the 'Green Zone'. Peter worked as an IT consultant, training local staff. On 29 May 2007, Peter and four British guards were kidnapped whilst at work. He was moved to Sadr City and transported onto Basra. He describes his first year as 'pretty rough', including 'mock executions, being hung over the door and regular beatings'. By 2008 Peter describes his conditions as 'better'. He was 'blindfolded and handcuffed, kept in a laying down position for six months and separated from the other four guards'. He later found out that all four guards had been shot and killed. At this point Peter was released from his chains, for the first time in two years. Peter said that at this time he hit his 'all-time low', and considered using the chains to hang himself. In 2009 he was 'given a laptop, was able to exercise, and had the use of a toilet'. This was the year he was released, on 30 December 2009, 946 days after he was first taken hostage.

When I asked what psychosocial support he was offered on his return, Peter informed me: 'My organisation did not have any, but after I was released from being a hostage the UK government had a military psychologist appointed to me.' Peter describes his main difficulties on his return as trusting people: 'when I was released I was introduced to a load of people who I had never met', and readjusting to life back in the UK: 'I actually did not return to the UK for six years. I went back to Guyana where I had been living and working before I went to Iraq.' He also struggled to get back into a day-to-day routine, 'my company wanted to send me to Afghanistan within a few months of being released. My only option was to quit the job, so I was not impressed with their lack of flexibility'. Peter also suffered a large dose of survivor's guilt.

Peter would recommend the following points be considered in a trauma management programme:

- Organisations need to have an in-house psychologist or psychological first aider; one main point of contact to support the member of staff. 'I was contacted by so many different people from the police, military, government. It was too overwhelming. This made me angry. I wasn't nice to deal with, but it all felt so intrusive and invasive.'

- Training for staff deploying to high-risk environments should be mandatory, including multi-day hostile environment training and at least a one-day hostage awareness course.
- 'A thorough assessment on my return and a phased return to work plan would have been helpful.' It can take a significant amount of time for someone to feel they can function well again and be productive, after a traumatic event. An occupational health assessment may be needed, reporting a clear return to work plan highlighting reasonable adjustments.
- Peter recommended a workplace debriefing for all staff returning from deployment. 'This approach could be taken like a review of the project, rather than being badged as something psychological.'
- Peter felt a buddying system would be helpful. 'A colleague could offer support, and if the individual needed further help they could be signposted to more specialist services.'
- He advised that it is important to listen to close family members and friends, if they feedback concerns about the way you are behaving: 'take them seriously as they are more likely to see the warning signs than you are'.

One way that is helping Peter to recover is to share his experience through presentations to humanitarian organisations and the military. He ends one of his talks with the quote from the German philosopher, Friedrich Nietzsche: 'That which does not kill us makes us stronger', and, at the same time, he also shares that his recovery has taken seven years to date, and is still ongoing.

Megan Nobert: case study

Megan Nobert, a Canadian aid worker, was deployed to the Gaza Strip, Jordan and South Sudan, where the focus of her work included humanitarian law and gender-based violence. While in South Sudan in 2015 she was sexually assaulted by another humanitarian worker. She went public about her experience in July 2015, and was also inspired to start an NGO called Report the Abuse. Megan shares some of her story with me below:

> If you experienced sexual violence in the course of doing your work, you would expect support from your organisation. You should be entitled to support. Sadly, this was not the case for me, and isn't for many other humanitarians.
>
> When I was drugged and raped while working for an INGO in South Sudan, I expected my organisation to provide an easy path to

getting medical and psychosocial support to provide the space and resources to heal, and to support my attempts to get justice. Instead, the opposite happened, in nearly every way. I fought my organisation to get the care that I needed. I begged for their help to get justice. I sent email after email asking for updates, contacts; asking them to care about what happened to me. When I asked for a week off to return home – to see some friends and tell my family what I had experienced in the field – I was told it would be disruptive to programming and if I wanted to go home I should quit. So I quit, to go home and heal.

There were many traumatising moments: When I was asked to go from room to room and relive my experience for senior management, because they couldn't sit together to hear from me. When I had to beg to stay in the guesthouse because senior management didn't want me there. When I was told that, if I wanted to be evacuated post-rape, it was my responsibility to make it happen. Beyond all of this though was the moment when I was told by senior management that I wasn't allowed to speak about my experience; it was the INGO's narrative, and things would be best if I stayed silent. If there had been policies or procedures in place, perhaps things would have been handled better. What I believe, however was that the essential missing piece was their lack of compassion and empathy. The absence of this – from my organisation and colleagues – was devastating. I've spent nearly two years trying to rebuild my ability to trust people with my story and emotions; a journey that will continue for some time. Speaking about it has helped, as has finding a group of fellow survivors. The wounds from how I was treated by my former organisation run deep, though; in some ways even deeper than those from the rape itself.

A clear trauma management programme for managers to refer to in the early stages after a critical incident is essential. How individuals are treated by their organisation directly after a crisis is fundamental to their recovery process; the 'stuck moments' in therapy can often be an unsupportive comment said by a manager or colleague. Individuals are highly sensitive and vulnerable to being re-traumatised in the early stages after an incident.

Megan would recommend the following points to be considered in a trauma management programme:

- A way to seek support without having to get permission or consult with HR, therefore enabling access to psychosocial support in a secure and confidential manner.

- A post debrief after the incident, carried out by an independent professional and in a compassionate and empathic manner.
- Continued care once humanitarians return home by way of regular check-ins and monitoring staff:

> Often, because of our work and the distance from home, going back can be as traumatic as being in the field. The trauma of what we see and experience might not be immediately evident either, it might take weeks or months to set in.

- Sexual violence awareness training to all staff in the preparation stage, including how to respond to sexual violence survivors, and confronting victim-blaming and rape myths.
- Established and clear procedures within a critical incident plan for managing sexual violence. These must be available in many languages.
- Setting out procedures for submitting reports or complaints of sexual violence.
- Establishment of an investigative or inquiry procedure.
- Safety and security management systems that address risks of sexual violence while working in the field.
- Creation of a whistleblowing network that allows reporting of sexual violence incidents without fear of reprisal.
- Advice and access to good quality medical and psychosocial care.

When I hear these stories, I start to question how detailed organisational critical incident policies are, and how often are they reviewed. Yearly simulation training of an organisation's critical incident plan should take place, such as the one offered by International Location Safety (ILS). As George Shaw, Director and Founder of ILS, describes, 'this crisis management training programme … tests systems and teaches managers the critical skills required to be a successful crisis management team member'. Knowing how difficult it is for managers to manage these situations, what support are they getting?

> Remember for the managers making the decisions it is always a tough call. It is a horrible feeling to be in a city waiting for a plane to collect people from the field fearing the worst. I can remember being on my knees in prayer once really struggling to hold it together while someone was about to be evacuated.
>
> (Ed Walker, former Programme Director of Tearfund)

Organisational trauma

When trauma impacts a member of staff, that same trauma runs through the veins of the organisation. Without the right trauma training and awareness organisations can start to act out of 'denial' and 'avoidance', as Megan's experience describes. These are symptoms of trauma. In psychological terms we call this systemic or collective trauma, depending on the circumstances. As Erikson, an American sociologist states:

> by collective trauma … I mean a blow to the basic tissue of social life that damages the bonds attaching people together and impairs the prevailing sense of communality. The collective trauma works its way slowly and even insidiously into the awareness of those who suffer from it, so it does not have the quality of suddenness normally associated with 'trauma'. But it is a form of shock all the same, a gradual realisation that the community no longer exists as an effective source of support.
>
> (Saul, 2014, p. 3)

Therefore trauma awareness training is not just for the staff deployed to high-risk environments, but also for the policy makers, senior management, human resources and security personnel.

> In our work with organisations, the employee assistance program CiC often refers to the 'ripple effect' of trauma that can quickly take hold across departments and affect the functioning of even the most mature organisations. Yet managers who are well trained in spotting aspects of the effects of traumatic events on their workforce will gain respect from their teams as well as feeling confident in their own leadership skills.
>
> (Nowlan, 2014, p. 11)

How do organisations make sure each staff member who requires psychosocial support receives it, particularly during a mass incident, and without overlooking support for national staff? Feedback from the 9/11 terrorist attacks on the Twin Towers in New York (Stuber, Galea, Boscarino & Schlesinger, 2006) and the King's Cross fire in 1987 in London (Turner, Thompson & Rosser, 1995) identified that individuals may have been underserved in terms of psychosocial support. Therefore, following the London bombings on 7 July 2005 international experts, who had experience of managing terrorist incidents in Madrid, Jerusalem and New York, were consulted. From gathering this up-to-date knowledge, a 'screen and treat' model was developed. This model was successful in generating more referrals of individuals than the normal channels would have achieved (Brewin, Scragg, Robertson & Thompson, 2008).

> The novel emphasis in the screen and treat program is primarily on the longer-term goal of identifying, following up [three, six and nine months], and screening all trauma-exposed individuals with properly validated measures to determine who develops persistent symptoms of psychopathology, and then giving them evidence-based treatment. The importance of outreach is underscored by reports that there is a particular low rate of treatment-seeking for PTSD, with fewer than 10% of affected individuals receiving any kind of help in the year after onset.
>
> (Brewin et al., 2008, p. 4)

This is highlighted in both Peter's and Megan's cases, above. They both left their jobs feeling unsupported and having not received good quality screening and treatment to help them in their recovery. Samid, another aid worker, agrees:

> I think after security incidents, psychological support and screening should be a mandatory step. When a member of staff has experienced an incident they are not necessarily in the best position to think clearly and request support. The process for me was not straightforward and required following up with Human Resources.
>
> (Samid, India)

The success of the screen and treat programme is highlighted in the recovery rates: '78% of those with PTSD achieved significant change in their post-traumatic symptoms, and these improvements were well maintained among those followed up after one year' (Brewin, Fuchkan & Huntley, 2009, p. 5). Therefore, it is important that any trauma management programme includes a screening process with longer-term follow-up.

What psychosocial support should be available to staff after a critical incident?

I have a great deal of empathy for organisations trying to design their own trauma management programme. Even for a psychotherapist, early intervention is confusing and greatly controversial. It reminds me of a day I participated on the International Location Safety (ILS) Security Awareness and First Aid (SAFA) course. The SAFA course is similar to a Hostile

Environment Awareness Training (HEAT), although it includes a greater awareness of the psychological impact of trauma. The course prepares staff to work in high-risk and hazardous environments, and utilises several simulation exercises, to enable the participant to have that essential hands-on experience. After two days of training and being prepared for any eventuality, I tentatively walked into the next simulation exercise, senses heightened, staying close to my team, watching out for any untoward movement in the undergrowth ahead of me. A couple of minutes into the exercise a team member (actor) screamed out in agony and we all became frozen on the spot; the ground below was littered with mines. Comparably, early post-trauma intervention can feel like a minefield to navigate. Below I have attempted to decipher the confusion and explain some of the controversy.

I would recommend that a trauma management programme include the following:

- immediate crisis management
- screening
- family liaison support
- peer support
- psychological first aid
- psychological debriefing
- initial trauma assessment
- specialist trauma counselling
- follow-up/closure.

The World Health Organization (WHO) and partners have developed the Inter-Agency Standing Committee (IASC) intervention pyramid for mental health and psychosocial support in emergencies (WHO, 2008). This model is a multi-layered system of support that meets the needs of different groups. It is depicted as a pyramid, with the wider lower end representing 'basic services and security', i.e. practical support needed to reach the wider audience. Moving up the pyramid there are three further sections: 'Community and family supports', 'focused, non-specialised supports' and, at the top of the pyramid, 'specialist services', which are required for a smaller number of people. The aim of the pyramid is to help countries match response strategies with community needs and appropriate expertise. In regards to a critical incident, immediate crisis management and practical support would be at the lower spectrum of the pyramid and possibly followed by peer support, whereas specialist trauma counselling would be placed at the higher level of the pyramid.

Immediate crisis management

The WHO emphasises four main themes for helping responsibly after a traumatic event: '1.) Respect, safety, dignity, and rights. 2.) Adapt what you do to take account of the person's culture. 3.) Be aware of other emergency response measures. 4.) Look after yourself' (World Health Organization, War Trauma Foundation & World Vision International, 2011, p. 8). If you find yourself in a situation where you are supporting staff that have been impacted by trauma or acute stress it is important you have good self-care strategies in place (see Chapter 4). The situation is often chaotic in the initial stages of a critical incident. Thus the immediate stage of any crisis is all about practical support, and de-escalating and defusing the situation. Five points to consider in the immediate crisis phase:

1   Safety and practical support: the immediate focus is on practical support, such as medical, environment, evacuation, social engagement and signposting. Have an understanding of the context and setting, and treat people according to their cultural and social norms.
2   Non-judgemental communication: individuals need to feel heard and supported. Refrain from using any terms that could be heard as judgemental.
3   Offer empathy, not sympathy: empathy focuses on understanding the perspective of the other person, whereas sympathy is placing our perspective of the situation on the other person.
4   Empowering: provide information and guidance, but allow the member of staff to make their own choices as much as is possible.
5   Information and administration: the administration processes can often be overlooked in the initial stages of a crisis, but it is crucial to have these processes up and running as early as possible to record all actions taken.

Screening

Most people will recover from a traumatic event naturally, but having an evidence-based screening process, one that is culturally and ethically appropriate, can monitor individuals who may need further support. Screening should be carried out on a regular basis, ideally within the first week following an incident, then at one-month, six-month and one-year follow-ups. This will ensure that all staff needs are met, including identifying staff that may experience a delayed reaction, and will supply the organisation with useful data. Trained and professional clinicians would ideally conduct the screening sessions using evidence-based questionnaires, which need to be comprehensive, and explore physical, psychological and social needs, including current support and resources available to the client, and assess risk. I have seen this assessment stage rushed, and, undertaken as what I perceived to be a tick-box exercise. Staff have been offered ten minutes to complete questionnaires and talk to a clinician, which is not acceptable. Not only does the staff member feel unsupported, it is also frustrating for the clinician. Ideally questionnaires would be completed pre-appointment, followed by a thorough assessment with enough time to cover psycho-education, normalisation and coping strategies.

It is worth considering regular screening processes for all staff deploying to high-risk environments. This precautionary measure can prevent individuals falling through the net of care when they may be struggling. Screening should include tools for assessing burnout, stress, anxiety, depression and trauma symptoms.

Family liaison support

Family liaison officers are necessary when a member of staff has died or they are unable to speak for themselves, perhaps through a kidnapping incident or being unconscious. This role often falls onto a senior member (or sometimes the only member) of the HR team. This is not appropriate for several reasons: the HR manager is often in the Crisis Management Team (CMT) (the family liaison officer should not be), the normal day-to-day running of HR becomes impacted, and it places an inordinate amount of stress on the person responsible for this role. I have seen many HR personnel burn out after juggling their HR role with the family liaison role. The family liaison officer's responsibilities include: being the point of contact between the family and the organisation, keeping the family informed, listening to the family's needs, providing practical guidance, signposting for further support where necessary, and helping the family deal with the reality of the situation. They should have additional psychosocial support available to them if necessary. In a world that is so reliant on media, social networking and other virtual communications, families need to be informed and supported as quickly as possible, alternatively they may come across information by other means, which can cause a rupture in the relationship between the families and the organisation.

Peer support

Peer support programmes are a great resource and support to national staff as they are versatile, cost-effective and can offer support to staff that are harder to reach. Peer supporters are volunteers within the organisation. They will be assessed regarding skills and resilience, before being trained and offered supervision. This training should consist of trauma awareness and psychological first aid, management of sexual assault, stress and resilience, and training of the trainer (where necessary). *Early social support is an extremely important mediator of recovery following a crisis* (Sphere Project, 2004; IASC, 2007). Steve Ryan, a security consultant, highlighted this when discussing peer support with me:

> Recent research suggests that PTSD is not just caused by singular traumatic events; cumulative stress can contribute to the disorder. For aid workers who witness or hear traumatic events daily, feeling supported and having people to talk to can be hugely beneficial. Whilst it can be difficult for an individual to know how to begin supporting colleagues, it is important to stress that we all play a part in creating a supportive environment. Making a real effort to interact with people meaningfully can open a channel of communication that goes beyond office small talk, increasing the likelihood that you will notice when something is wrong.

It is often colleagues that notice the first signs of a peer struggling and are well placed to offer early psychosocial support, and by doing so, can improve an individual's recovery.

Psychological first aid (PFA)

PFA was first developed by Raphael (1986) and is seen as the foundation of psychosocial response to a major incident. PFA can be delivered to a group or individuals, and encompasses safety, information, emotional support, psycho-education and access to further services, if necessary (Brymer et al., 2006). It supports people while respecting their dignity, culture and abilities, and helps individuals identify their needs and natural coping strategies. Many international and national expert groups have recommended PFA, including the WHO, IASC and the Sphere Project.

There is overwhelming evidence demonstrating that social cohesion is a major protective factor following trauma (Hobfoll et al., 2007): 'In the early stage of emergency, social supports are essential to protect and support mental health and psychosocial wellbeing' (IASC, 2007, p. 1). Judith Herman, Professor of Clinical Psychiatry at Harvard University Medical School, explains in more detail the importance of social cohesion in the healing process after a traumatic event:

Traumatic events destroy the sustaining bonds between individual and community. Those who have survived learn that their sense of self, of worth, of humanity, depends upon a feeling of connection with others. The solidarity of a group provides the strongest protection against terror and despair, and the strongest antidote to traumatic experience. Trauma isolates; the group re-creates a sense of belonging. Trauma shames and stigmatizes; the group bears witness and affirms. Trauma degrades the victim; the group exalts her. Trauma dehumanizes the victim; the group restores her humanity.

(Herman, 1997, p. 214)

Group support services are one means of offering a vital ingredient of social cohesion. Therefore a support group offering containment and safety will enable individuals to share their experiences, which in turn encourages healing and closure. The risk to the organisation of not offering a psychosocial support group after a traumatic event is that individuals take longer to recover, and harbour angry feelings towards the organisation.

PTSD symptoms from a previous trauma were exacerbated when a colleague was shot and killed on our compound. A counsellor was called in to one of the hubs to talk with staff but we were actively encouraged by management to just move on and not talk about it. For 'smaller' incidents like staff members being attacked or being held at gunpoint no support was offered.

(Akash, Bangladesh)

PFA is 'a humane, supportive response to a fellow human being who is suffering and who may need support' (World Health Organization et al., 2011, p. 3). PFA offers a chance to triage and assess staff. The advantage of PFA is that peers can be trained to facilitate groups, making it an economical and accessible option. Reports from providers suggest that PFA is well received (Allen et al., 2010), although, as with psychological debriefing (see below) further research is still needed to prove its effectiveness. The difference between PFA and psychological debriefing is that PFA can be activated whilst a crisis is ongoing (i.e. national staff working and living in a conflict zone) and can be activated soon after a crisis, while psychological debriefing (below), is offered after an event has ended. PFA offers psycho-education, normalisation and resourcing. Psychological debriefing takes a further step in trauma recovery by enabling participants to create a narrative and meaning of the incident.

Psychological debriefing

Psychological debriefing (Dryregrov, 1989) was developed 30 years ago for organisations whose employees are exposed to traumatic material. After the Cochrane review (Rose, Bisson, Churchill & Wessely, 2009) psychological debriefing was labelled 'harmful', with 'watchful waiting' of symptoms recommended instead (NICE, 2005, p. 5). It was suggested that asking individuals to tell their story of the traumatic event would re-traumatise them. This has made offering psychological debriefing controversial, leaving humanitarian aid organisations and the psychotherapeutic professions perplexed. Many clinicians have now found the original research to be flawed (Hawker, Durkin & Hawker, 2011), including the British Psychological Society (BPS), which is now challenging NICE, after holding two symposiums on early trauma interventions. I continue to see a great demand for this psychological debriefing in the humanitarian aid field. Organisations such as emergency first responders, the fire brigade, the police, Employment Assistant Programmes (EAPs), NHS foundation trusts, various NGOs and United Nations departments are continuing to use various forms of psychological debriefing. Additionally, the Substance Abuse and Mental Health Services Administration (SAMHSA) have endorsed psychological debriefing (Tuckey & Scott, 2014).

Many clinicians have concluded that 'watchful waiting' in itself could be harmful and that the articles referred to in the Cochrane review had methodological limitations (Dyregrov & Regel, 2012), for the following reasons:

- Debriefing was carried out on individuals it was not originally intended for.
- The timing, length, training, and independence of the debriefer did not follow the CISD protocol.
- The focus was on individual debriefing, whereas the original model was developed for groups.
- The groups that were debriefed had more severe symptoms than those who were not debriefed.

Some conflicting research has found that debriefing has been associated with a significant reduction in alcohol misuse among British soldiers (Deahl, Srinivasan, Jones, Neblett & Jolly, 2001). Mitchell and colleagues have identified other benefits such as improved coping skills, increased morale and staff retention, reduced sick leave and compensation payments, and reduced usage of mental health services in the 12 months following the incident (Mitchell & Everly, 1997; Robinson, Mitchell & Murdock,

1995). In the research for this book, 90 per cent of aid workers that completed the questionnaire stated that they would want psychological debriefing to be offered to them following a traumatic event.

A popular model of psychological debriefing is Critical Incident Stress Debriefing (CISD) (Mitchell, 1983). This model was specifically designed for emergency workers following distressing events, and created as a group support model. Alternative models of debriefing developed including the Trauma Risk Management (TRiM) protocol, which was developed in the Marines. This approach is a peer support model where the participants focus on facts, feelings, and the future after a traumatic event, and includes an assessment of ten risk factors (Greenberg, Langston & Jones, 2008). Other adapted models focus participants on the facts, thoughts, reactions, symptoms, future planning and disengagement of the incident, and less so on feelings. The participants begin to create a group narrative of the event, and find a common meaning.

Hawker (2016) writes that good psychological debriefing should entail:

- Experienced and qualified debriefers who have an understanding of the organisational culture.
- Assessment of how the groups are setup and who attends which group, taking into consideration group dynamics.
- Sessions no shorter than two hours, with follow-ups available.
- The awareness that debriefing should not be carried out within the first 24 hours.
- Facilitation only once the crisis is over.
- Voluntary participation; debriefing should not be mandatory.

Initial trauma assessments

Some staff members may choose not to attend a psychosocial group, or it may not be beneficial to them, depending on the nature of the traumatic incident. Therefore an initial individual trauma assessment, which can be carried out remotely, and covers elements of the PFA model, can be helpful. A trauma assessment needs to include identifying symptoms, normalising, and enabling the individual to recognise and develop coping strategies. It creates a space for the individual to talk through their experiences, and can offer a monitoring process and follow-up appointments if necessary. It may even be that a one-off trauma assessment is all the individual needs to feel supported, or they may be referred on for further specialist support.

Specialist trauma counselling

The NICE guidelines state that:

> Trauma-focused cognitive behavioural therapy should be offered to those with severe post-traumatic symptoms or with severe PTSD in the first month after the traumatic event. These treatments should normally be provided on an individual outpatient basis. All people with PTSD should be offered a course of trauma-focused psychological treatment (trauma-focused cognitive behavioural therapy [CBT] or eye movement desensitisation and reprocessing [EMDR]).
>
> (NICE, 2005)

Both TF-CBT (Ehlers, Clark, Hackman, McManus & Fennell, 2005) and EMDR (Shapiro, 2009) have been culturally adapted to be effective globally although many countries do not have access to specialist trained therapists in these approaches. It is therefore useful not to overlook other trauma therapies that are also getting good results globally, such as Narrative Exposure Therapy (NET) (Schauer et al., 2005), and the Tree of Life Model (Denborough, 2008). Additionally, many clinicians offer these services remotely through various software applications and webcam.

Follow-up/closure

It is good practice to offer follow-up appointments one month, six months and one year after a traumatic incident, so staff feel that their experience of having been through a distressing situation is acknowledged, and that they are supported and valued by their organisation. However, in most organisations the resources for this will be limited. I have often heard about group debriefings being carried out with no follow-up. This can leave individuals feeling frustrated, and lacking confidence in future psychological services. 'My organisation were excellent in offering psychological debriefs after difficult deployments. It helped us to feel closer as a team and we felt the organisation was taking our wellbeing seriously' (John, UK). I supported a team of staff who had lost one of their team members in a car crash. They were a close team and were great at supporting one another. They requested that I came back a year later to facilitate a group event in regard to the one-year anniversary of their colleague's death. Anniversaries and specific dates of events are important to note, and can be triggering for individuals. Also, if the incident was high profile, media may rerun footage of the event and produce documentaries, which can also be triggering.

Appropriate timings of offering psychosocial support

I would advise being aware of feeling a need or urge to offer immediate psychological services following an incident. Although this is often supportive for the members of staff that are managing the incident, it can feel intrusive to the individuals who have been directly impacted upon. For example, when a group of falsely imprisoned staff returned home and disembarked their plane, their families and counsellors were waiting for them. Some individuals found this helpful, and others did not. It is important to give individuals who have just experienced a traumatic event choice, as this enables a feeling of empowerment and being listened to. Working within crisis response I have received many calls from managers or HR personnel anxiously demanding that 'we need counsellors here now'! My role is to contain the anxiety and manage the situation by grounding and stabilising the individual on the end of the phone.

Difficulties to mental health clinicians also arise when they are requested to attend an incident directly as it unfolds, which can often occur. 'Well-intentioned, mental health practitioners should not "parachute" uninvited into a disaster zone, particularly if they have no knowledge of the local culture, language, mores and religious sensitivities' (Alexander, 2015). Counsellors or peers trained in trauma awareness, PFA and crisis response can be helpful in these early stages, but specific counselling is not, and when counselling has been activated too soon it has given the profession a bad reputation. This has resulted in over-dramatic headlines such as, 'Don't offer counselling to terror survivors – it could make trauma worse' (Donnelly, 2017). Of course, timings of offering the appropriate support are important, as we don't want to interfere with individuals' natural healing processes, but these types of articles tend to confuse people. Radio Five Live called me after the London Borough Market terrorist attack in June 2017, asking me to explain what this headline meant, as individuals had become frightened to reach out for any form of psychosocial support.

As highlighted above, timings around offering all the above-mentioned services can be difficult to navigate; there are great variants around the guidance regarding what services to offer, and when, within trauma services and research. Generally it is not advisable to offer trauma interventions in the first three days after a traumatic incident, as individuals are often in the shock phase. Some models would suggest offering debriefing after 24 hours, others up to one week. Trauma specialist counselling is usually offered one month after the incident, according to the *Diagnostic and Statistical Manual of Mental Disorders* (DSM-5) (APA, 2013). I have produced a table to summarise services that need to be considered in a trauma management programme, alongside guidelines for relevant timings (see Table 5.1).

Table 5.1 A trauma model for psychosocial services and relevant timings

Stages	Timings	Support services
CRISIS	Immediate	Crisis management Practical support: medical, environmental factors and reassurance. Move to a place of safety. Support and guidance. Social support. Signposting Peer support programmes Peer supporters trained in trauma and PFA
STABILISATION	1–4 weeks	Screening: individual assessment/triage/ evaluation Psychological first aid (PFA) (3 days +) Normalisation, psycho-education, resourcing Initial trauma assessments (3 days +) PFA, psycho-education and normalisation of symptoms can be offered, including building coping strategies Group debriefing (CISD) Finding a narrative and meaning (less focused on feelings at this stage) Continued monitoring for individuals that may need specialist support. Only offered once an incident has ended
PROCESSING	4 weeks +	Specialist trauma counselling One-to-one sessions can start earlier than four weeks if the initial stages focus on stabilisation. The trauma processing part of therapy tends to start after four weeks
INTEGRATION	Recovery period	Follow-up/closure Post-traumatic growth

Note
This table is the author's interpretation of early intervention support from reflecting on research in the field, and 15 years of personal experience working with trauma. There is a demand for the above services, which, if carried out professionally and appropriately, will help support individuals and groups after a traumatic incident.

Summary of early interventions

In short, it is essential for all organisations to have a critical incident plan, which needs to be tested annually through simulation training. A trauma management programme needs to be in place, which incorporates specific psychosocial needs for sexual violence and kidnapping and hostage-taking incidents. Assessment and triage need to be carried out early on after an incident takes place, and administration processes are important to set up during the immediate response. This enables all staff to be accounted for and makes sure that any staff who may be identified as 'at risk' can be signposted to appropriate specialist services. PFA can be a useful model to offer psycho-education, normalisation and resourcing for staff after an incident, and peer support programmes are also worth considering, so appropriately trained staff are available and at hand to support their colleagues immediately during a crisis. Psychological debriefing would not be activated until the incident has ended. If individuals are identified with ongoing psychological difficulties after four weeks, there are excellent trauma specialist therapies available, which are becoming more widespread globally through various training projects (see Chapter 7). Support for families needs to be included in the critical incident plan, providing information sheets – as needed – and family liaison support when necessary.

> An organisation must know what it does and doesn't have access to before the crisis hits. It needs to have the right people trained and ready to go when the moment comes and a plan in place. There won't be time to build that structure or develop that plan once a kidnap has happened.
>
> (Rudge & Regel, 2014, p. 12)

However, none of the above services should be mandatory as it is important to enable the individual to feel empowered after a traumatic event and, therefore, try to engage them in the decision-making process. I have experienced organisations offering group support, as it is more economical. I understand the financial pressures, but this cannot be the sole basis of the decision-making as the risk of poor early intervention can lead to further problems, including lack of productivity and sickness absence.

Psychological first aid and early trauma interventions are based on common-sense ideas, offering individuals social cohesion, coping strategies, compassion and empathy. These principles make a significant difference to an individual's recovery process, and can considerably reduce the time it takes for them to recover and heal. Megan and Peter did not receive this basic care, and were often re-traumatised by their post incident experiences. As Steve Ryan, security consultant, poignantly states, 'be a humanitarian to your fellow humanitarians'. I shared my story of suffering PTSD with you in Chapter 2. When I was in the ambulance and regaining consciousness I found a young woman sitting next to me. I had never met her before; she was a bystander in the street, and decided to accompany me in the ambulance. She stayed by my side until I was moved to the hospital ward. I never saw her again, and at a later date I did try to find her to say thank you, but to no avail. The memory of her presence, her compassion, and the moments she reached out and held my hand, comforted me through the darkest times of my PTSD. Christoph Hench (ICRC) also shared his story with me (see Chapter 1):

> During the first twenty-four hours, I felt that both the worst and the best sides of humanity were revealed to me. Once my colleagues dis-covered me in my room, lying in my bed, injured, there was not a minute where there was not someone present next to me, someone in touch – literally. Feeling that caring presence, with a hand on my arm or shoulder all the time, gave me a sense of grounding and infinite safety. I'm still grateful today to the nurses and all the others who accompanied me on that first day. But that sense of grounding, con-nectedness and presence started to evaporate only about twenty-four hours later, once I had arrived at the hospital in Geneva where the bullet was removed from my body.
>
> (Hensch, 2016)

Incorporating a clear trauma management programme into the critical incident plan supports staff through each stage of their recovery. Without referring to this ongoing trauma programme the wounded individual can become isolated and forgotten about, especially when the media hype dies down. This is why it is crucial for organisations to have a well-formed, and rehearsed, psychosocial wellbeing programme. The next chapter focuses on a consistent psychosocial support programme from the pre-, during and post- stages of a deployment, which covers the 'the complete package of care'.

6 The complete package of care
The road most travelled

> I have worked for over 25 years, within many organisations, and only one has offered any decent assistance, and that was only one session. Contrast that to the excellent support given to carers of cancer patients through Macmillan (something I have also experienced) and one realises how far behind aid organisations are. Having said that, there is no doubt that there is a reticence for people to seek this sort of help, which is almost certainly a cultural thing. During the Ebola crisis … South London and Maudsley (NHS) provided psychosocial care for up to 12 months following the medics' return home, but take up was very low, despite the obvious mental trauma they experienced with a patient loss rate that, at times, was over 70 per cent.
>
> (Jon Barden, humanitarian advisor, contractor working for DFID)

Stigma is still preventing individuals reaching out for psychosocial support. Some of the comments on the questionnaire included, 'If I ask for psychosocial support it will affect my career', 'I will be judged as weak and may not be asked to go on certain deployments' and 'we are expected to just get on with it and not complain'. Kadesh, an aid worker of over 22 years, shared her story with me:

> I went straight from a job in South Sudan to a position with the West African Ebola response. About six months on from the Ebola response I was burnt out – just completely exhausted and had terrible insomnia, felt like I was constantly ill, and no longer had any drive or interest in my work. I ended up taking a few weeks of unpaid leave, using the excuse of wanting to be home for the holidays, as there was no clear way to explain to a supervisor or HR that I was burnt out without feeling like I would risk my job.

When we review the history of trauma, stigma has played an injurious role, with traumatised women and soldiers being labelled as 'hysterical' and 'moral invalids', respectively, resulting in punitive and harmful trauma treatments. During the First World War, soldiers who we now understand as having been traumatised were referred to as suffering from 'shell shock' or having 'low moral fibre', and were perceived as hysterical and weak, resulting in them being ridiculed, punished and even shot for desertion. Many of these punitive treatments would re-traumatise patients. After the Second World War it became more recognised that anyone could be impacted by 'war neurosis', not just those perceived as weak, which resulted in more humane treatments emerging. In the early 1970s two groups developed that made a significant difference to how traumatised individuals were treated and perceived. The two groups were 'Rap Groups', organised by the 'Vietnam Veterans Against the War', and 'consciousness-raising groups', led by the women's movement and set up to support women who suffered sexual violent crime. These groups were fundamental in raising awareness of trauma symptoms. Both groups refused to be stigmatised and silenced, which resulted in funding finally being granted for further research into understanding the impact of trauma on individuals (Herman, 1997). After decades of stigmatised oppression and punitive treatments, recognition was granted and, in 1980, a diagnosis of post-traumatic stress disorder (PTSD) was published in the *Diagnostic and Statistical Manual of Mental Disorders* (DSM) (APA, 2013). Some clinicians would argue against labelling or pathologising individual's mental health difficulties. While I can see both sides of the argument, having suffered PTSD and having treated hundreds of individuals with PTSD, I do believe that this diagnosis was fundamental in creating aware-ness, funding, research and specialist trauma treatments. We know that in many countries those suffering from trauma symptoms are still stigma-tised, still punished and still re-traumatised by inappropriate and cruel treatments, or have no access to specialist support.

Could organisational culture be changed to challenge this stigma? I joined Transport for London's (TfL) Trauma and Counselling team after the 7/7 bombings in London, July 2005. Pre-7/7 TfL as a company was known for its macho, male-dominated culture, and stigma was a significant hurdle in preventing individuals from reaching out for psychosocial support. Due to the substantial number of staff that needed trauma treat-ment post-7/7 this stigmatised culture started to shift, as staff began to refer themselves for trauma specialist counselling. A trauma support group volunteer programme was developed, training peers in psychological first aid skills to support colleagues in the immediate aftermath of a crisis. Senior managers spoke of their own struggles and openly attended psycho-social support programmes. Concerns regarding the stigma of mental health issues within organisations arise year after year at global mental health conferences, with well-intentioned, passionate speakers sharing their experiences and learning. But the rate of change is agonisingly slow, and as each year passes there is risk of more staff causalities as individuals become 'burnt' by their work.

I was presenting alongside Jon Barden, humanitarian advisor, in the symposium of 'helping the helper' at the Global Mental Health conference at King's College in London, in June 2017. Barden's talk, 'Better to burn out than fade away', painted a picture of his personal stories whilst he was working in Afghanistan during the 1990s, which were laced with traumatic events. One of these traumatic incidents resulted in Jon and three national staff being held at gunpoint. They stopped at a checkpoint as they were driving towards Logar, where several guards piled into their vehicle.

> We passed through the small village and drove up into the mountains for about ten minutes when the guy in charge ordered us to stop the vehicle, and we were dragged out by our hair and told to go and line up in front of a large rock face. I told my guys to sit down where they were, as I didn't think we should make it easy for them to shoot us impersonally with the heavy machine gun. We all sat down spread apart by about thirty feet or so, and everybody's attention was on our driver who was sobbing and grabbing the ankles of one of the gunmen. I had a guy next to me who cocked his Kalashnikov, pointed it at my forehead and gabbled at me in Dari. Since I didn't understand what he was saying I took a look around me and contemplated that I was going to die, that no one knew where we were and that it was going to take ages to find our bodies. I decided that the only option was the last cigarette of the condemned man. I lit up and suddenly had three guys round me all asking for a cigarette. I gave them the packet and my Zippo. They all took one, lit up and politely gave them back to me. I said 'I thought you were going to kill me so what are you giving these back for?' They, of course, looked at me blankly.

Jon and his colleagues survived their ordeal. 'The thing I am most proud of is that without any training, and so acting on instinct alone, I saved the lives of myself and three Afghans operating entirely through an interpreter.' Although they survived physically, Jon was burnt by his experiences and suffered PTSD.

> I related the tale to our acting country director, who told me that I was lucky because two of the world's leading PTSD researchers worked out of Peshawar and she would call them. Five minutes later I was told they were both on leave and that I would be going to see a

psychiatrist in Islamabad the next day. I went and a very nice person told me that she had read an article about PTSD and would send it to me. She then asked me what I thought I needed. I said a couple of weeks' holiday after which I could draw a line under the incident and life would go on as normal. She agreed and I was sent to Bangkok (our six-monthly R&R destination) for two weeks. About five months later when my actual R&R was due I went to ask about getting it booked, and was told I had already had my R&R and would have to work for another six months without a break. For about a month after the incident I would be dropping off to sleep and would suddenly be jolted wide-awake by the sound of the Kalashnikov being cocked. When I did sleep my dreams were full of the most horrendous accidents, resulting in massive amounts of blood and gore.

After Jon shared his personal story I followed with my presentation, 'Trends in critical incidents for aid workers', where I could share some of the advancements made in offering psychosocial support to aid workers since his experiences. Although there have been improvements in challenging stigma, developing trauma awareness programmes, and increasing access to psychosocial support, I believe that overall the humanitarian sector still has a long way to go in offering best practice psychosocial support to prevent their staff from getting 'burnt'.

This chapter will describe various means of psychosocial care, which I hope will urge organisations to create a 'road most travelled', consistent and clear pathway of support for staff. I encourage the reader to review each stage and consider what is needed to support staff in relation to their deployment. For those deploying to a high-risk environment, I would recommend an overall pathway of care that supports aid workers through the pre-, during and post-deployment stages. Preparing staff pre-departure, being available to provide support whilst in the field, and following up with them post deployment is crucial in promoting staff wellbeing. If these pathways become the norm they will help to break through stigma, and encourage individuals to reach out for support when they need it.

The provision of support to mitigate the possible psychosocial consequences of work in crisis situations is a moral obligation and a responsibility of organisations exposing staff to extremes. For organisations to be effective, managers need to keep their staff healthy. A systemic and integrated approach to staff care is required at all phases of employment – including in emergencies – and at all levels of the organisation to maintain staff wellbeing and organisational efficiency.

(IASC, 2007, p. 87)

United Nations Human Rights Council's (UNHCR) staff welfare recognises that the ideal state of the workforce is 'high engagement and high wellbeing'. It offers a three-fold approach to psychosocial care, which I will be exploring in this chapter (UNHRC, 2013):

- individual and group counselling for those experiencing difficulties;
- capacity building and training pre- and during deployment;
- peer support personnel network.

Pre-deployment psychosocial support

Too many aid workers are being deployed without appropriate training. I read a blog from an aid worker whose first deployment was to South Sudan. She had little preparation and training through her induction process, and was asking other aid workers for advice. Many responded with concern that South Sudan would be her first deployment (this was soon after the 'Terrain hotel' incident in Juba in 2016, where several aid workers were attacked and raped). I read many helpful and realistic recommendations in response to her post, whereas others claimed that the recommendations were 'scaremongering'. I found this an interesting discussion, as I would always promote realism when preparing an aid worker for deployment. As Aideen Lucey, an organisational resilience consultant who also spoke at the King's College conference, stated, 'the strength is in engaging with the difficulties and not avoiding them'.

One specific difficulty was the urgency to deploy aid workers when the Ebola crisis started in 2014. Staff were assigned to Sierra Leone, Liberia and Guinea, with little preparation time, while deployments of staff already working in these countries were extended, to maximise staffing levels. Further staff, who were new to international work, were deploying from within the NHS. As a result of the Ebola crisis, Public Health England has now set up an emergency response team, which will train staff in advance so that they can deploy within a 72-hour period.

> It's not enough to be trained in technical know-how, in disease surveillance, setting up treatment centres – it is also vitally important that such specialist emergency response workers are prepared psychologically for their task – that they are fit and healthy and psychologically resilient so that they can effectively respond to the next lethal health threat and go on responding in the future.
>
> (Dr Simon Clift, Consultant in Occupational Medicine)

Trauma needs to come with a warning. Television programmes warn the viewer if they are about to show violent or traumatic material, so that the viewer can decide whether to watch it or not. Where I supervise staff in a suicide prevention organisation, part of the resilience building practices I promote includes adding a warning before sharing traumatic material with colleagues. We need choice and we need preparation time before being exposed to traumatic material, as this helps to reduce the psychological impact. As the Latin phrase 'praemonitus praemunitus' translates, 'to be forewarned is to be forearmed'.

Annabel came to see me for trauma counselling after she visited a small village in Zimbabwe, where she was handed a dead baby by one of the mothers from the village. She was asked to say a few words in front of the extended family. Apparently her predecessor had experienced the same situation twice. Annabel had not been informed of this, and believed that if she had been forewarned she would have coped much better. Adelene, who deployed to Sierra Leone after the Ebola outbreak, wrote:

> I think it should be a recommendation for employees to undergo a pre-deployment mental health check when going to conflict or emergency countries, during which employees have the chance to chat through what they think they may witness during their trip. This may go some way in preparing them. I feel like part of the issue with my deployment was that I had no idea I would be spending a week on a maternity ward in the maternal mortality capital of the world. Had I of known this before I may have been able to prepare myself mentally.

Mandatory security training is now part of the pre-deployment preparation. Many organisations now insist that all staff attend a refresher course every three years. Psychosocial hazards should be treated with the same importance and urgency as physical surveillance, in order to support organisations to meet their duty of care to their workforce (Acas, 2012). Therefore I would strongly advise that the same procedure be in place for trauma awareness training, and in fact many individuals, through the research for this book, requested that trauma awareness training be annual.

> The team leaders and managers need to be fully aware of the signs of stress, and mental health issues, and know how to deal with staff empathically. They need to make sure all their staff know what is available, and empower them to access it.
>
> (Almut, Germany)

Staff at all levels should attend trauma and stress awareness training. If staff at the top of the chain are traumatised, burnt out or stressed, this becomes contagious and creates a ripple effect all the way down the chain of command.

> I think the least that should be offered is information sessions to all staff on possible reactions to incidents and possible psychological support available. Anything that can help staff recognise and identify that they might be suffering from trauma or PTSD would be helpful pre-deployment.
>
> (Bijan, Iran)

Some of the training courses to consider when preparing staff for deployment read as follows:

- Trauma awareness: to provide an understanding of trauma symptoms, and the physiology and neuroscience of trauma. Being able to recognise the signs of trauma or burnout in others, and ourselves. To gain skills in supporting someone who is traumatised.
- Vicarious trauma: understanding how we can be impacted vicariously by traumatic events or traumatic material. Building coping strategies and practical skills in self-care.
- Psychological first aid (PFA): to equip aid workers with the basic knowledge and confidence to provide robust material and psychosocial support to colleagues and team members in the immediate aftermath of a traumatic event. PFA training is offered in peer support programmes, as I mentioned in the previous chapter.
- Stress management and resilience building: to identify our stress cycle and build our resources to manage our stress levels. Practical exercises to reduce stress, including mindfulness, movement and meditation.
- Sexual violence awareness: to enable participants to better protect themselves against the threat of sexual violence, and be better placed to respond in the event of an incident occurring. To define sexual violence, challenge myths and build skills to support a colleague after a violent sexual crime.
- Kidnapping and hostage-taking survival: to gain an understanding of the psychological effects of kidnapping and hostage-taking. To be aware of the different processes of a kidnapping and hostage-taking scenario, and what goes on behind the scenes. Exploring the challenges of, and strategies for, readjustment and reintegration.
- Hostile Environment Awareness Training (HEAT)/Security Training and First Aid (SAFA): to equip humanitarian staff with skills to prevent and respond to the most prevalent security threats they face, in the course of their duties in insecure environments.

- Critical incident training: a simulated training programme that tests an organisation's critical incident plan and teaches managers the critical skills to be a successful crisis management team member.

The International Community of the Red Cross (ICRC) and Save the Children are offering some of these trainings online, and Humanitarian Outcomes is also developing an online training module. 'Practical, "demystifying" humanitarian training allows new aid workers to do their job more efficiently and effectively, and feel more included from day one of a response, vastly reducing this one area of stress' (Shane, South Africa). Meanwhile, 'inadequately oriented and trained workers without the appropriate attitudes and motivations can be harmful to populations they seek to assist' (IASC, 2007, p. 81).

Organisations need to explicitly inform their staff about the psychosocial support that is available. This information needs to be easily accessible through induction packs, user-friendly websites and psychosocial e-learning programmes. Information needs to be given on what in-country support is available in a crisis. 'I feel psychosocial support should be displayed and explained frequently and in lots of different places, both in buildings but also online. Also managers should understand it and talk about it freely' (Luka, Croatia). When carrying out pre-deployment consultations I ask staff what support is available to them, and many will answer that they don't know or that there is none. I remember working in a large government-run organisation. I was visiting an office to discuss and promote psychosocial support to the manager of a sizeable group of staff. Although he implied he was supportive of the psychosocial services we could offer, he refused to place the information leaflets in the main office, stating that 'I will refer a member of staff to the services if they are struggling, but I don't want to encourage it'. One aid worker said that:

> I think providing secure and confidential psychosocial support in a variety of languages should be the norm, not the exception. Everyone has different levels of trauma tolerance, and a one-size fits all approach won't work. Some staff might not need therapy, others might need a lot. In order to create a healthy humanitarian workforce, seeking help must be normalised.
>
> (Marco, Switzerland)

Most appointments can be carried out face-to-face or remotely, which enables national and local staff to have equal access to these services. These appointments are ideally set up by external organisations, so as to promote objective assessment, and become part of the organisation's processes and procedures. Staff have requested a 'named' individual that they can contact throughout the pathway of psychosocial support. This is possible whether internal or external services are provided, and is something organisations should consider.

> I think organisations should provide mandatory pre-deployment psychosocial briefing sessions where staff can share any concerns, discuss coping strategies, and develop a relationship with a counsellor. During their deployment, that counsellor should be the one consistently available to support them at a distance.
>
> (Annabel Morrissey, Conflict Advisor)

These appointments have been referred to as 'psychological clearances', 'pre-deployment assessments' or 'pre-deployment resiliency and stress management consultations'. Pre-deployment consultations could be included as part of the 'Management of Health and Safety at Work' (1999) legislation, which states that: 'Every employer shall ensure that his employees are provided with such health surveillance as is appropriate having regards to the risks to their health and safety which are identified by the assessment.' Most of these appointments cover the same factors, such as emphasising resilience and recognising strengths; identifying risk issues and any vulnerabilities; exploring unprocessed traumas or mental health concerns; psycho-education, including stress management; assessing and building on resources and social support; reflecting on current challenges, and/or concerns of deployment. Some organisations will require reports from these pre-assignment consultations. 'I think a psychosocial session should be provided pre-deployment, to de-stigmatise mental health care. It would also serve to help equip humanitarians with tools needed to get through their mission mentally healthy' (Azad, Bangladesh).

Having carried out hundreds of these consultations, I have found individuals invest different levels of enthusiasm and dedication during these assessments. Some individuals perceive them as a tick-box exercise; others really invest in learning about themselves and how they can improve their coping strategies when on deployment. Some individuals gain insight into why they might behave a certain way in specific situations, and they can start to explore how they might change those behaviours, if it is beneficial for them to do so. Some staff make use of the session to discuss and implement a self-care plan and explore setting healthy boundaries. Ninety per cent of aid workers who completed the questionnaires stated that a pre-deployment consultation should be available to all staff. I would take this a step further and recommend that pre-deployment consultations become part of an annual medical health check, which would include reviewing the past year, looking at any challenges, struggles or difficulties, and also acknowledging what went well, therefore offering a key resource for reducing the effects of cumulative trauma and stress.

Psychosocial support during deployment

A mid-deployment review may have been recommended during a pre-deployment consultation, due to certain risk issues being identified, for example previous mental health vulnerabilities or current and ongoing lifestyle issues, such as the ill health of a family member. Alternatively, a traumatic event may have taken place and staff may be requesting additional support, or someone may be suffering from stress, anxiety or burnout. 'If in a challenging environment, I think it would be useful to have a monitoring or checking-in session, so staff are forced to take time and think through their current state of mind' (Maan, Syria). Alternatively, if an individual is deployed to a high-risk environment this may be set up as a pathway of care, so that they would automatically be booked in for a mid-deployment review.

> I would suggest that organisations provide three monthly check-ins that are semi-mandatory with counsellors. Most people I know would refuse to have help and struggle to reach out, but potentially if something is built in, there is a proportion of people that would use that.
>
> (Ibrahim, Mali)

If a pathway of care, which includes a pre-, mid- and post-psychosocial consultation, becomes the norm, it will normalise and challenge the stigma that prevails throughout organisations.

> If you make the mental health support something routine and regular following incidents, it takes away the stigma and makes it easier for people to ask for help/have any issues identified as soon as possible. In my experience, after a traumatic event, seeking help is overwhelming and terrifying. By setting it up so that it is automatic and someone reaches out to the individual instead of making the individual do the reaching out I think more people would use mental health resources.
>
> (Yosef, Israel)

The mid-assignment consultations cover factors such as reviewing the self-care plan (if one was made); identifying the stress cycle and ways to manage stress levels; identifying symptoms and monitoring and assessing the level of difficulty; help with building motivation and increasing energy levels, and signposting or referring onto specialist services if needed.

> If you have a three-month assignment then you get a psychosocial debrief. But if you are on a three-year assignment you still only get one in the middle or after a critical incident. They should be mandatory after every year.
>
> (Ed Walker, former Programme Director of Tearfund)

If a mid-term review was requested after a traumatic event, services may include psychological first aid or psychological debriefing, depending on the type of incident and who has been impacted, and provide ongoing support if necessary. Many aid workers found it helpful to have a named individual to contact if an incident had occurred that required the need for further support.

> Part of the problem when I was on deployment was there was no named person as a point of contact for me to talk to. We had a security check-in every 24 hours, but I think during this time it would be useful to check on the mental health of a person too.
>
> (Mariel, Philippines)

Post-deployment psychosocial support

Post-deployment consultations have been named 'post-deployment debriefings', 'confidential reviews', 'personal impact reviews', 'end of assignment sessions' and 'post-deployment resilience and stress management debriefings'. Post-deployment consultations enable the member of staff to process experiences from the deployment, explore and debrief any difficulties that may have arisen, discuss things that went well, acknowledge individual and team strengths, recognise motivations and meaning gained from the work, discuss resilience levels and wellbeing, find closure of challenging events, develop a personal transition plan if needed, and review next steps. Additional factors include identifying any risk issues including the onset of burnout, stress, anxiety or trauma, and signposting and referral to specialist services if necessary.

> I think it should be a requirement that employees undergo psychological screening post deployment. I think this would allow employees to feel it's part of a procedure rather than them having to ask for one and feel like they're making a fuss, which can often be the feeling among employees.
>
> (Hamid, Pakistan)

One hundred per cent of aid workers who completed the questionnaires for this book stated that post-deployment consultations should be available to all staff. 'I think a post-deployment debriefing with a counsellor should be mandatory. It would help if all staff had to do it to support those who may not have the courage to request support' (Rose, Nigeria). Should post-deployment consultations be compulsory? I saw many staff who were psychologically impacted after the Ebola response, but it was identified that the uptake was low for post-psychosocial support. At InterHealth we introduced an 'opt out' process, which seemed to encourage more individuals to attend post-deployment appointments. Therefore, I would recommend an 'opt out' option, although it is worth reviewing which individuals are opting out. Someone may be identified as 'at risk' or 'struggling' and choose to opt out. It may be worth checking in with this individual to monitor how they are and their reasons for opting out of a post-deployment appointment, as some individuals develop an avoidant coping strategy, that may hinder them reaching out for the appropriate support.

> At the very least a post debrief gives all staff the sense that their opinion is valued and therefore provides a boost to self-esteem. Additionally, organisations will learn from their own staff what they should change for the next response.
>
> (Luca, Switzerland)

Generally, post-deployment sessions are confidential, although some organisations may require a short report.

> It comes down to access with stigma and without the sense that accessing such services might jeopardise progress or future contracts with that organisation. Perhaps this means that the access needs to be fully confidential without any report having to go to the organisation. Hard to guarantee, especially since a person with PTSD is often the last to admit they have it, and might be a danger to colleagues or themselves in extreme cases; something which an organisation should be told.
>
> (Ester, Burundi)

Post-deployment reviews should be offered to anyone who has experienced a distressing or traumatic event whilst on their deployment.

> I recommend routine post-deployment reviews for all staff, regardless of whether there was a specific security incident during their deployment or not. Even on 'normal' deployments we end up dealing with

emotionally heavy issues and really should be spending more time addressing the impact this has on our mental wellbeing. We need to make access to support something that is just routine and normal, or else no one will really use it.

(Ed Walker, former Programme Director of Tearfund)

I supported a group of staff after a critical incident in Africa. When the staff returned home, and a recommendation was made for two individuals to receive counselling, the manager told me that once employees return home the organisation would not normally continue caring for them. I was shocked by this response, given that the volunteers had suffered a workplace trauma.

All organisations need to decide on their approach to the routine provision of mental health care for staff who are found to suffer with significant mental health disorders. For those conditions which can be clearly understood as a psychological injury related to an occupational role (e.g. mental ill health following a serious accident at work) then strong consideration should be given to ensuring that affected individuals are provided with evidence based care in a timely fashion and whether, and for how long, financial support from the organisation should continue.

(Dr Simon Clift, Consultant in Occupational Medicine)

The homecoming

The homecoming is often an overlooked phase of someone's deployment. Indeed, many individuals find returning home, and the effects of reverse culture shock after an assignment, more difficult than deploying. I have also heard individuals struggle in this readjustment phase, stating their 'normal jobs' don't have the same level of responsibility, or kudos, as the role they had when working overseas. I've experienced individuals feeling 'guilty' for having fun, after the things they witnessed during deployment. Going back to 'normal' life can begin to feel 'mundane'. Having a pathway of care and support that extends through pre-, during and post-deployment will help individuals return as resilient as possible. However, for some individuals there can be a delayed response, the NICE guidelines (2005) suggest this could affect 15 per cent of individuals impacted by a traumatic event.

During a deployment an individual can be running off adrenaline. Therefore, when they return home, and things begin to slow down, their body starts to feel the impact.

It is sometimes hard to come back from a mission, especially when it lasts for several months and in a totally different culture. After a mission in conservative countries, it can be difficult to go home and be able to dress up like before. Contact and proximity with others can be difficult. There is also the feeling of being lost once back home, having a difficult time going to the grocery and knowing what to do, what to buy, what to eat.

(Vanessa, Spain)

It would be helpful to send all staff returning home a basic fact sheet of what to potentially expect when they return, with some stories of what other people had experienced. I also think that a post deployment briefing is essential. However, things are normally fine in the first three months, it's normally later that people struggle and at that point struggle to reach out to the services provided by the organisation.

(Annabel Morrissey, Conflict Advisor)

As individuals we also often neglect to prepare for the transition back home. Dave Pollock refers to the acronym of a trip on a 'RAFT' in regard to the returning home process, 'for the raft to arrive safely, it must be durable' (Schuppener & Schuppener, 2016, p. 24). He refers to the raft being made up of four logs:

1 Reconciliation: consider making a last attempt at any reconciliations to resolve any outstanding problems during the goodbye-phase.
2 Affirmation: reflect on what you have appreciated during your time away, the good times and learning from the bad.
3 Farewells: consider parting rituals and farewell celebrations, not just with the significant people you have met, but also specific places or animals. Being forced to leave a place suddenly can leave a sense of non-closure. A post-assignment debrief can also help individuals find closure.
4 Think destination: take time for some realistic thinking about what awaits you back home. How are you going to communicate about your deployment? How much detail do you want to share? Who might be the people you can reach out to for further support?

I've not been home for more than a couple of weeks in the past four or five years but whenever I am on leave it is stressful to cope with the disparities between the issues I work on while on deployment, and what life is like back home. It is hard to communicate with friends and loved ones in a way that is honest about what I deal with, but doesn't scare or upset them. I can't exactly talk about being held at gunpoint or having mothers die from lack of healthcare the same way they talk about the latest TV shows. I find myself saying things that they just can't relate to and neither they nor I know how to handle it. It perpetuates the feeling of being cut off and not having the necessary support to really deal with emotional and mental health in a healthy way.

(Stan, Holland)

It is important to watch out for colleagues that you think might be struggling. Warning signs might include excessive alcohol, nicotine or caffeine intake, and recreational drug use; displaying emotional or aggressive outbursts; seeming on edge; becoming easily triggered into reactive behaviours; becoming isolated or overworking; expressing thoughts of hopelessness, or losing one's passion or motivation; appearing distracted, confused or preoccupied; experiencing lots of physical ailments, or looking tired, mentioning difficulties with sleep or relaxing.

When returning from Sierra Leone I really struggled for a number of weeks settling back into my old life. I would go out and get drunk a lot to try and forget about what I'd witnessed while on deployment. Sometimes I felt quite isolated as I felt no one could quite understand what I'd seen. I'd be on public transport and suddenly burst into tears for no reason, which was really unlike me as I'm normally a really emotionally stable person. I often had nightmares and flashing images of certain moments from my trip, which I couldn't get out of my head. That's when I knew something was wrong and that I needed to seek treatment.

(Antonio, Spain)

As much as a staff member who is going on their first assignment may be seen as at risk, due to lack of experience, additionally a member of staff who has carried out over five deployments could be monitored as at risk, as they may be more prone to burnout. Research was carried out on soldiers in regard to how many months they spent in combat, and showed correlation between the more months spent in combat, over a three-year period, and progressive decrease in the alpha power at the back of the brain, which is associated with relaxation. This area of the brain regulates elementary processes, such as sleep and hunger.

The decrease in alpha power in these soldiers reflects a state of persistent agitation. At the same time the brain waves at the front of the brain, which normally have high levels of beta, show a progressive slowing with each deployment. The soldiers gradually develop frontal-lobe activity that resembles that of children with 'attention deficit hyperactivity disorder' (ADHD), which interferes with their executive functioning and capacity for focused attention.

(Van Der Kolk, 2014, p. 324)

Therefore the symptoms of ADHD can be indicative of developmental trauma, such as trouble concentrating; forgetfulness and difficulty organising thoughts; fidgety and manic behaviour; and being easily distracted. Developmental trauma refers to childhood traumatic events that still impact us and causes us to experience trauma symptoms, particularly impacting our relationships and significant attachments. Some clinicians would argue that ADHD is, at times, a misdiagnosis of developmental trauma. Furthermore, many of the warning signs and symptoms mentioned in the above few paragraphs could be related to vicarious trauma, which has also been referred to as secondary trauma or compassion fatigue. Vicarious trauma can have a cumulative effect, and is the residue of the exposure to traumatic material.

It wasn't until I ended my deployment and was working somewhere else that I fully realised how traumatised I was by continually seeing colleagues and local populations being victims of violence. I had gotten to a point where I just couldn't absorb the level of violence that I shut down and stopped processing. Once I was removed from the situation it took a few months to realise that I was experiencing vicarious trauma.

(Hani, Ethiopia)

Conclusion

Organisations need to create a 'road most travelled' pathway of psychosocial care; a pathway that becomes part of the preparation phase and duty of care throughout the entire time of a staff's deployment, particularly for staff deploying to high-risk environments. The pathway of care needs to include pre-, during and post-psychosocial interventions, as well as specialist services after a critical incident, and ongoing monitoring. The last two chapters have examined a 'trauma management programme' within a critical incident plan, and the full package of psychosocial care pre-, during and after deployment. Having good practice guidelines for supporting staff psychologically creates a resilient organisation, reduces turnover and sickness levels, and increases staff motivation and loyalty.

Unfortunately, critical incidents will continue to occur and aid workers are at risk of being targets of an attack. However, we can help staff recover well, and we can help staff to feel supported by their organisations.

Thinking more widely, what is best practice psychosocial and trauma care in less resourced countries, in countries that don't have a language for psychological trauma, and in countries where healing is focused on the community as a whole, rather than a western view of healing the individual? It is important that all these considerations are reviewed, and cultural differences are taken into account, when working internationally. The next chapter explores some of these questions and considers the importance of 'do no harm'.

7 Cultural relevance of psychosocial support

Local roadmaps

In this chapter I will explore many facets of the cultural relevance of psychosocial support – including access to culturally sensitive support – and its associated challenges; the development of local mental health services and the consequent challenge of using Western norms and staff, as well as the disparity of care between national and international staff. 'Addressing stressors and preventing harm from inappropriate emergency responses is essential to promote and protect psychosocial well-being, prevent distress and, possibly, to prevent disorders, and to ensure that community ownership and protective safeguarding mechanism are in place' (IASC, 2017, p. 17).

Cat Carter (Save the Children) shared her experiences of the difficult stories she had heard over the last five years, and how the cumulative exposure to trauma had led her to suffer from PTSD. At a TED talk in 2015, Cat told the story of a young girl in Gaza, aged five, named Nada. During a bombing raid her parents had asked Nada and her siblings to sing at the top of their voices to drown out the noises of the bombs. That day Nada witnessed the death of her family members. She became mute from then on.

> That is something that is seared on her brain forever. That's just one story that I heard from my time in Gaza, one of hundreds, if not thousands, of stories of children that I have heard over the last five years, and each one, I feel, is also seared onto my brain.

Cat goes on to explain that Nada received therapy from two Palestinian therapists.

> They introduced a new, fascinating type of therapy, that is remarkably simple … and it involves a balloon … she can't talk, so normal therapy does not really work for her, so they give her a balloon, and

they say to her.... Think of everything that is upsetting you today, all of that hurt, and that grief and that fear about what happens next, and blow it all into the balloon.... They then tie it up and give it to her. It is up to her what she does with the balloon. Sometimes she just sits and looks at it and cries, sometimes she puts the balloon away to think about later ... but sometimes she finds the strength to pop the balloon, and just for that one day she has managed to move past her grief.... The counsellors said to me the reason they think it works, is that it tells her 'your feelings are important and they matter, it was a huge thing that you went through and suffered and it has changed you and you will never be the same again, but it hasn't defined you and it is up to you now what you will do with those feelings; you can take back control'. One of the overriding emotions children in these types of emergencies experience is the utter loss of control. They have no control over whether they will be shot, tortured or bombed.... By doing this, it gave back a sense of control, autonomy and power, to do what she wants to do.

(Carter, 2015)

There are many creative ways of offering culturally sensitive psychosocial support that respect difference, disability, culture, religion and context. Nada has access to therapy sessions, but many countries have limited access, if any, to psychosocial services. This book covers best practice trauma care and offers guidance on implementing an organisation's trauma management programme. Many of these services are universally applied, but consideration needs to be given to specific context and culture. The Red Cross developed a psychosocial framework, based on the mnemonic 'CALMER': Consider, Acknowledge, Listen, Manage, Enable and Resource (Davidson, 2010). This framework was piloted with different populations in various countries, and supports the Red Cross's Diversity Agenda. Therefore, it has been designed specifically to acknowledge people's differences and to consider how to attend to these when establishing trust and developing supportive, healing relationships.

Culturally sensitive support

In many countries, individuals would see a spiritual leader rather than a mental health professional for their psychosocial support needs. It is important therefore to incorporate spiritual and cultural practices and meaning when developing a trauma treatment programme. Many cultures place greater emphasis on community and family support compared to western cultures, where the focus of psychological services can be seen as individualistic. What local resources are already available? What are the cultural rituals for people to express grief? What are the local coping strategies? Inka Weissbecker, mental health adviser for the International Medical Corps (IMC), notes that 'in Ethiopia people say depression is related to loss ... so the community takes up a collection and they all give them something' (Leach, 2015). She refers to group therapy sessions that incorporate local practices such as praying before and after, as this is something the women wanted to do.

Established theories and principles, for example karma theory in South Asian localities, can provide an existing framework that should be taken into consideration when considering the individual experience of traumatic events. Within karma theory, the individual, family and community may believe that a traumatic event has happened to an individual due to karma from an earlier life event, or something that their ancestors may have done. As a young woman from Myanmar said to me, 'this can stop the cycle of destruction, as you do not consider revenge; you accept this has happened to you due to previous life experiences'. However, at the same time, a man who had been tortured for many years said that 'karma can also stop people reaching out for help, or talking about their experiences, as it can bring shame to the family'.

Nonetheless, challenges do exist when developing trauma treatment programs outside of western contexts, given the complexity of language and psychosocial terminology. Many countries do not have a word for 'trauma'. Whilst delivering a trauma training in Myanmar, the nearest translation I could find for the word 'trauma' in Burmese was 'saint dan ya', meaning 'injury of the mind'.

Cultural models of psychosocial support

EMDR and TF-CBT have been adapted to work effectively globally. Research has concluded that the augmentation of CBT with spiritual and religious beliefs has shown the increased effectiveness of this therapy in western and non-western cultures (Azhar, Varma & Dharap, 1994; Razali, Hasanah, Aminah & Subramaniam, 1998). Trauma Aid UK (formerly known as the Humanitarian Aid Program [HAP]) recognises the lack of specialist trauma care in many countries and has therefore offered *pro bono* training in traumatology and EMDR to local mental health professionals in over 30 countries. There are many European EMDR organisations, in Germany, Spain, Italy, France and Holland. They have conducted projects in China, Indonesia, Ukraine, India, Palestine, Pakistan, South America and Cuba.

The ethos of HAP UK & Ireland is the 'teach a person to fish' prin-ciple.... The aim is that, in countries and regions where we embark upon projects, local mental health professionals are supported over a period of up to five years in their education, training and development in the treatment of trauma, particularly EMDR, so that they, in turn, can train their colleagues and compatriots. Eventually we anticipate that countries will be able to found their own EMDR national and regional associations. This has already taken place in an ongoing project begun in 2009 in Bosnia-Herzegovina.

(Abdul-Hamid, Hacker Hughes & Morgan, 2016, p. 4)

EMDR Asia was established in 2010, and its current goal is to establish an EMDR Middle East and Africa.

Experiencing a traumatic event can challenge our existential meaning of life, and therefore religion plays a significant part in making meaning and purpose of our life, whether we turn to it for support or against it during times of crisis. Jamie Hacker Hughes (past BPS president and clin-ical psychologist) and Walid Khalid Abdul-Hamid (psychiatrist and clin-ical director of Priory Wellbeing Clinic) presented a paper that suggests the ritual movements associated with the Sufi Dhikr may involve a form of Bilateral Stimulation (BLS) as conducted in the therapeutic trauma model of EMDR. Sufism (a mystical trend in Islam) and other spiritual beliefs and religions constitute important aspects of the person's resilience and ability to cope with trauma and stress (Abdul-Hamid, 2011; Dein, 2006). Hughes and Abdul-Hamid are exploring ways of incorporating Sufi Dhikr into a modified EMDR protocol. 'We anticipate that this would give EMDR an even wider and more popular acceptance in the Middle East and the Muslim world' (Abdul-Hamid & Hughes, 2015, p. 150). EMDR therapy is widely accepted and used globally, in America, Europe, the Middle East, Africa, Asia and Australia (Maxfield, 2014). EMDR has been used in humanitarian crises, as it is effective as a brief individual interven-tion, consecutive-day application, and group therapy model. Group EMDR protocols are seen as valuable in certain circumstances, such as mass dis-asters, where there are large numbers of victims and few clinicians. It appears to be useful for reducing anxiety, strengthening coping resources, and screening for those who may require further individual attention. EMDR Recent Traumatic Episode Protocol (R-TEP) (Shapiro, 2009) developed by Elan Shapiro, can be used to support individuals within one month of a crisis.

EMDR proponents say the therapy is well-suited to humanitarian crises like disasters and war, in which large populations are dealing with trauma and may be moving from place to place for safety. Advocates say it works fast ... and can be used in groups without requiring people to discuss their experiences in detail.

(Alfred, 2015)

The intensity of EMDR means results can be achieved in hours and days, rather than months and years. Individuals have found this to be culturally sensitive, as they do not need to talk about the incident in detail.

As much as existing cultural systems can be seen as congruent to western therapeutic practice, other philosophies themselves have also fed into the development of western therapy, highlighting that the cultural sensitivity of delivering western therapy is not a one-way relationship, but that there can be symbiosis in existing approaches. There are many eastern healing traditions such as tai chi, yoga, Emotional Freedom Technique (EFT) (tapping meridian points located in the body), painting, play, and group activities such as community acting, singing, music and sport. I have incorporated traditional symbolism into my work, for example in using sky lanterns from Southeast Asia, featured in festivals and celebrations, which have been historically emblematic to summon help. They also represent the carrying of prayers or wishes, and are symbolic of hope. Tibetan prayer flags, some named 'Lung ta' which translates to 'wind horse', represent peace, compassion, strength and wisdom. The prayers and mantras will be blown by the wind to spread the good will. Elan Shapiro adapted his EMDR protocol to include the four elements (Shapiro, 2009). Earth represents grounding and reminds the individual to practice grounding exercises. Water represents calm and control, and encourages individuals to drink water, activating their digestive system. Air represents breath, and encourages individuals to practice relaxation and mindfulness. Fire represents imagination, and reminds individuals to practice visualisation exercises. Many of these techniques work well cross-culturally, they can work with individuals, groups and communities.

The metaphor of a tree has been adapted for several therapeutic models, including the 'Tree of Life' developed by Ncazelo Ncube-Mlilo and David Denborough (Denborough, 2008), which originated in South Africa, and the Blob Tree (Wilson & Long, 2009) model. The Blob Tree incorporates images of people/blobs within a tree, which are neither male nor female, young nor old, rich nor poor. Individuals are asked to identify which one represents them and why. This model initiates conversations about emotions for cultures and groups that would not comfortably open up about their feelings. These therapeutic models increase resources, resilience and social connections. Professor Mooli Lahad, founder of the Community Stress Prevention Center (CSPC) in Israel, specialises in trauma care.

Lahad developed a trauma model, SEe FaR CBT. SE meaning Somatic Experiencing, FR for Fantastic Reality/playing with imagination, and CBT, Cognitive Behavioural Therapy. I observed him use picture cards to help a traumatised individual begin to create a narrative of their experiences. He works in a creative way using pictures, puppets and movement. Lahad's work is accepted globally, and he presents on culturally sensitive post-trauma treatments.

Peer support has been mentioned throughout this book as a sustainable and economical option for psychosocial support for national and local staff. UNHCR staff indicated that they rely most heavily on peer support in times of distress (Welton-Mitchell, 2013). As Leanne Kennedy, CEO of Thrive Worldwide, shared with me:

> the goal of peer support is in developing systems and practices that develop internal sustainability around wellbeing. If staff are being supported on a regular, on-going basis, the goal is that wellbeing is improved, the impact of chronic and traumatic stress is mitigated, and the need for specialised services is reduced.

Training volunteers in psychological first aid facilitates peer support, because it means staff can receive direct support from colleagues. This will help to reduce longer-term mental health issues. Staff can also be signposted to specialist support services if needed. The Inter-Agency Standing Committee (IASC) recommends that organisations,

> train some staff in providing peer support, including general stress management and basic psychological first aid. For national staff who may be unable to leave the emergency area, [they should] organise access to culturally appropriate mental health (including psychiatric) and psychosocial support and physical health care.
>
> (IASC, 2007, p. 90)

Implementing peer support programmes into an organisation's ethos can challenge organisational stigma often associated with mental health. Social media sites for aid workers also create a supportive social network (although seem to be more heavily used by international staff), such as 'Fifty Shades of Aid', Global Aid Worker and Humanitarian Women's Network. The Headington Institute and Antares Foundation also have excellent wellbeing resources that are easily accessible from their websites (see 'Sources of help' for further resources).

Developing localised services or importing international professionals

Arukah Network is a global network of local people who work for sustainable, community-led health and wellbeing. Its diverse membership is united in a belief that every community has the gifts and skills it needs to achieve health and wellbeing for all its members.

> When development is based on naming a community's problems and then getting outsiders to try and solve them, then development can define local people as incapable, it can diminish their prior achievements, and it can discourage their future initiative. On the other hand when development starts with local people coming together to take stock of their own skills and abilities then development becomes part of a much wider process. One that builds stronger relationships, that forges better leaders, that kindles an entrepreneurial spirit, and that improves the health of a whole community.
>
> (Arukah, 2017)

For trauma recovery to take place communities need to feel useful, valued and empowered.

Angela Byrne, a clinical psychologist, presented at the Global Mental Health Conference at King's College, London, in June 2017. Her talk, entitled 'Why I decided to stop working internationally', highlighted her concerns about the 'west knows best' approach and her concerns about the risk of harm being wrought by – albeit well-intentioned – people intervening in cultural contexts with which they are unfamiliar. 'It is important to incorporate and utilise approaches originating from developing countries, such as traditional healing and faith healing. These approaches may represent affordable, acceptable, culturally appropriate, and effective strategies for managing stress.' She goes on to emphasise that individuals should not be working internationally if they don't feel competent doing the same work back home. Psychosocial clinicians should not offer their services unless they are competent to work cross-culturally and have advanced skills of working in trauma and crisis support.

Sarah Davidson, head of psychosocial services at the Red Cross, also highlights the importance of checking the assumptions that underpin our actions.

> By not checking with those with whom we are working, we risk causing harm through our assumptions, by being misguided or blinkered, such as offering individual therapy rather than engaging a

family, community or organisation; or by offering assistance through an inappropriate channel, such as a mixed-gender group.

Additionally, Davidson notes that 'each stakeholder must be placed on an equal footing, avoiding some of the more colonial attitudes and power imbalances traditionally seen in the relationships between richer donors, who have exported aid and dominant ideologies, to poorer beneficiaries' (Bayne & Jinks, 2013, pp. 280–281).

We are also aware that access to psychosocial resources and specialist help is limited in many countries.

> Mental illness is one of the great invisible health issues in all societies, accounting for four out of the ten leading causes of disability worldwide. Yet in low-income countries, there is an average of just one psychiatrist for every two million people and psychologists or social workers are also in short supply. During emergencies the percentage of those suffering common mental disorders doubles from 10% to 20%, while those with pre-existing and severe mental illnesses often have no access to care.
>
> (IMC, 2017)

Therefore, peer support and the EMDR 'teach a person to fish' ethos can help provide a country with sustainable psychosocial services, as demonstrated in the following example:

> During the horrific war in the Democratic Republic of Congo (DRC) during the years 1996–2007, a research group conducted an evaluation study of the use of an intervention program carried out by trained local staff. Results showed that using local staff not only reduced the cost but increased the use of the program, particularly by trauma victims and sexual assault victims. Training local staff enhances cultural awareness and the provision of appropriate services for the diagnosis and treatment of trauma victims.
>
> (Abdul-Hamid & Hughes, 2015, p. 151)

The DRC has a limited psychosocial support infrastructure and therefore these projects enable staff some access to support services.

There are times, however, due to lack of resources, when it is helpful to implement external sources of expertise.

> There has too often been an assumption that counselling is not culturally relevant and that local staff would not make use of this 'western'

practice. When counselling is offered, [organisations] soon realise just the opposite is true. Local staff readily and enthusiastically make use of these services to deal with stress, anxiety and the other challenges of intense and often high-risk work.

(Hess, 2017)

My experience of offering in-country psychosocial support to local and national staff in Gaziantep in Turkey throughout 2016, while working at InterHealth Worldwide, aligns with this quote. Within the humanitarian organisations, where I provided the service, 85 per cent of the staff were made up of Syrian refugees and Turkish staff. There was demand and uptake for psychosocial services offered. I also experienced national staff as being eager for information and keen to learn about psychosocial topics. The assumption that local staff will not utilise and appreciate this support can be short-sighted, and can reinforce a culture of stigma against mental health issues. This does not overlook the fact that psychosocial treatments need to be culturally sensitive and appropriately adapted to suit the context.

In July 2016 alone, InterHealth was contacted by 26 humanitarian organisations requesting support in South Sudan after attacks by government soldiers on local people, aid workers and anyone caught up in the indiscriminate attacks of violence, raping and looting. Clinicians at Inter-Health, who supported national staff based in South Sudan, facilitated psychosocial support programmes. A stepped psychosocial model of care was offered, facilitated by clinicians that had good knowledge of the cultural considerations, which consisted of group work combined with offering one-to-one appointments, if requested. The South Sudanese staff were less inclined to take up the offer of one-to-one appointments. This could have been due to the cultural desire to discuss events and issues communally rather than individually, or that the referral system involved informing management, which is not ideal. These programmes of support were kept flexible so as to meet the cultural needs of the national staff. Information was provided in various languages, training was adapted to take into account cultural differences, and translators were on hand if needed.

There remain clinicians that are critical of diagnostic labels such as PTSD, and the globalisation of individualistic interventions. Trauma symptoms are often seen as a way for the body and mind to protect itself and is an important part of recovery, therefore this process is a natural healing process, and some would suggest, not a disorder. There is a great deal of debate as to whether the PTSD diagnosis is helpful within a non-western culture: 'the instruments used in the vast majority of past surveys have not been validated for the culture in which they have been applied, which creates further uncertainty over how to interpret results' (IASC, 2007, p. 45). The Impact of Events Scale (Weiss, 2007) was used for both projects in Gaziantep and South Sudan, to assess and monitor trauma symptoms. The scale was not used as a diagnostic tool, however it was referred to as a discussion and normalising tool for the symptoms of trauma, to explore what is a healthy response and to highlight that most people recover from trauma naturally.

Through this work, although I found staff had a good understanding of stress management, there was limited understanding of the impact of trauma and trauma management. Staff found this information extremely useful and it helped them to make sense of what they were experiencing and why. Some of the feedback received included, 'I'll be more under-standing to everyone in my organisation', 'We should work very hard to rescue the people of South Sudan from stress and trauma and conduct this training all over South Sudan, because South Sudanese are suffering from trauma' and 'I learnt to be more peaceful by listening to myself'. High levels of trauma symptoms (suggesting a diagnosis of PTSD) were recorded for 41 per cent of the Turkish and Syrian staff, and for 53 per cent of staff based in South Sudan. National and local staff experience high levels of trauma symptoms, depression and anxiety; often living and breathing trauma every day whilst trying to survive in warzones or conflict-ridden environments, and also coping with everyday adversities, such as lack of food, clean water and access to medical care. Lack of security and a deteriorating situation has a great impact on the mental health of a population.

The key stressors reported for the Turkish and Syrian staff included: the Syrian conflict, workload pressure, domestic violence, traumatic health, developmental trauma, and instability and transition. For the South Suda-nese staff the key stressors included: complex bereavements, missing family members, displacement of self and family members, beating and violence, child malnutrition and fear of infant mortality, and marital and family breakdown. On the contrary, the key resources for staff included 'work' and 'relationships with colleagues', which enabled 'a sense of belonging and comradeship'. There was evidence of high levels of resili-ence and motivation, side-by-side with high levels of trauma symptoms. Spirituality and community strengthened resilience. Individuals often felt more passionate about the work they were doing. 'My work here is a good thing', 'I feel safer and more confident in myself during working hours', 'Work provides meaning and motivation'. One of the organisations increased organisational resilience by senior staff attending individual sessions, challenging stigma and role-modelling good self-care. On the contrary, damage to organisational resilience can take place when there is no follow-up support offered, and we found that even when we would recommend this, organisations would rarely implement it. Therefore the importance of peer support, building collaborative working with local services, or training local services (if necessary), enables psychosocial support to become accessible and continuous, rather than a 'tick box' exercise, that can leave staff feeling resentful and perplexed.

Weissbecker adds that one-on-one therapy with expats can help people who have experienced extreme violence, rape or torture.

> Some of them want to talk to foreigners because they don't trust people in their communities.... So then it's also important for them to have that one-on-one option.... The response to mental illness in many countries is often harmful.... Psychotic patients are chained. Children with developmental disorders are at risk of abuse. Mothers with depression have a higher risk of malnourished children. People with anxiety are often given benzodiazepines, which can be very addictive. The solution ... is to bring together global and local expertise.
>
> (Leach, 2015)

I also hear many stories of dehumanising, cruel and re-traumatising treatments of people suffering acute stress or PTSD, such as individuals being tied to chairs for hours on end, locked in rooms and labelled 'crazy', shot for being raped, ostracised from communities for having HIV. I offered counselling to a female Somali aid worker who had been gang raped. She said:

> I am the lucky one. I escaped. My brother was also raped and he is at home, and rocks back and forth in his chair all day. He can't tell anyone or he will be shot. There is no help for him.

Misunderstood trauma can be perceived as someone being cursed or under the influence of witchcraft, therefore culturally sensitive education and awareness of psychosocial issues becomes fundamental to cut the chains of this cruelty.

Ian Ridley, a senior director of World Vision, sums up well the balance between developing local services or importing international professionals, by stating that we should be striving for a humanitarian response which is 'as local as possible, and as international as necessary' (Wall, 2015). Antares recommends that 'The agency has standing arrangements with local, regional and international specialists during a crisis period to provide culturally relevant trauma assistance as required' (Antares, 2012, p. 28). I am often surprised at how many 'responding in a crisis' calls I receive, where organisations ask me what in-country mental health support is available. Surely finding out this information should be part of the induction and risk assessment process? Although we cannot predict or prevent all critical incidents, organisations that are knowledgeable of local services, engage in collaborative working, offer peer support programmes and training, and have access to specialist international services when necessary, can go a long way in helping prevent staff from suffering trauma and acute stress, and aid successful and timely recovery.

Supporting national staff

Even though there is a greater ratio of national staff verses international staff, the disparity of funding continues to be significant. The ACT Alliance Humanitarian Policy and Practice Advisory Group's (HPPG) Position Paper for the World Humanitarian Summit (WHS) called for 'Secure innovative, flexible and increased financing for locally-led responses, with a target of 20% of humanitarian funding channelled directly to national actors by 2020' (ACT Alliance, 2015, p. 2). There is also a shift towards better recognising and valuing local and national staff's abilities, capacities and needs. The 'Shifting the Power' project is part of the UK Aid-funded Disaster and Emergency Preparedness Programme (DEPP) and is being delivered by six international organisations. 'Shifting the Power' is a move towards developing and utilising locally owned and led responses, in order to support local organisations to strengthen their capacity to determine and deliver humanitarian preparedness and responses (Shifting the Power project, 2016). This shift encourages a healthy and inclusive way of working, but also emphasises the imperative to align psychosocial support for national staff with that which is provided for international staff. Kate Tong, a humanitarian consultant, shared with me that she has experienced a welcome shift, 'national staff are certainly in higher positions now than ever before, and more national staff become international staff so the whole global cadre of aid workers has become a lot less "white and western"'. The challenge is how to ensure all staff receive fair and equal access to psychosocial support, no matter where they live or what their culture. The eighth Core Humanitarian Standard (CHS) stipulates that 'Staff are supported to do their job effectively, and are treated fairly and equitably' (CHS, 2015, p. 4). Unfortunately, we are seeing that this is not the case when it comes to supporting local and national staff, whether by disparity in pay, leave, benefits or access to medical and psychosocial services.

Local staff working in conflict contexts are exposed to risk and trauma on a regular basis and often carry baggage from having grown up in a violent conflict context or having been a refugee from a young age. We seem to completely ignore this fact and apply such double standards. Over the last two years I've had desperate messages from colleagues in Afghanistan completely traumatised from sitting through attacks near their house, holding their children, praying they survive; or colleagues having to suddenly flee Juba and not knowing how to get their family to safety. We also had incidents of partner staff having to flee Kunduz when the Taliban took the city, being too traumatised to return and then being fired by their national organisation. I also remember after the earthquake in Haiti, how staff themselves were understandably traumatised and were returning home at the end of the day to a makeshift shelter under a bed sheet; yet we expected them to be 'on it' and full of energy to help respond to others and didn't even provide basic tarpaulins for them, despite the fact they were having to distribute them to other communities. It seems to me unacceptable that we expect staff just to be our agents on the ground and yet, as a people-centred organisation, build in minimal provisions for their welfare.

(Annabel Morrissey, Conflict Advisor)

I took a 'responding in a crisis' call from a manager when four of his staff members were raped in Zimbabwe. The two international staff were offered psychosocial support, and we were informed the national staff had declined any support. I was told that 'they turn to their family and community for support', but I later found out this was not the case, as the two young women felt afraid to share their experiences with their family or community, stating this was due to stigma. We cannot assume, in any case, what is best for the individual. That is why monitoring and follow-up are such an important part of a crisis response. In some cases, individuals can rely on their communities and families to support them, but this varies in regard to the context, nature of the crisis and many other complex factors. While in the field I have experienced that in some countries a traumatised individual is seen as a community problem, and together people find a solution, whereas in other countries individuals who have experienced a rape, for example, may be ostracised from their communities, and perceived as bad and dirty. Additionally, the IASC guidelines on Mental Health and Psychosocial Support recommend: 'Humanitarian organisations should work to improve their performance in staff support and to reduce differential support practices for national and international staff' and to 'promote inclusive and non-discriminatory service delivery, avoid unnecessary institutionalisation of people with mental disorders, and respect freedom of thought, conscience and religion in mental health and psychosocial care' (IASC, 2007, p. 51).

On 11 July 2016, several international aid workers were attacked in South Sudan, Juba in the Terrain Hotel complex. South Sudanese troops went on a four-hour rampage, shot dead a local journalist, and raped and violently attacked other aid workers. One of the international women who was repeatedly raped said:

> we survive, we are whisked out of the country and given treatment, we have access to counselling, we are taken back to our homes, which are in relatively stable parts of the world; we're looked after. It is a horrific experience and a traumatic thing to recover from…. For the women of South Sudan that experience rape, in a much more violent way, and much more often … they didn't get the chance to leave.
>
> (BBC Newsnight, 2016)

Many individuals are suffering from trauma in silence, particularly the trauma from sexual violence, which shrouds individuals in unsolicited shame. The data I gathered over the last three years from the responding in a crisis work at InterHealth highlighted sexual violence and kidnapping and hostage-taking incidents had increased. As I was seeking data on sexual violence against national staff I realised how little information was available, and the utmost need for further research. There are many reports on rape used as a weapon of war, against men and women, to dehumanise, humiliate, ethnically cleanse and spread disease. The Report the Abuse online survey completed by aid workers highlighted that 72 per cent of participants were survivors of sexual violence (Nobert, 2017). Unfortunately, the figures for national staff completing the survey were low. The Headington Institute noted that one in ten aid workers who came to them for support reported sexual violence (Jones, 2015). Studies of sexual harassment and assault against aid workers have noted that sexual violence was further compounded through an individual's sexual orientation 'Lesbian, gay, bisexual, and transgender (LGBT) aid workers reported sexual identity harassment, blackmail, threats, and assaults against them, primarily by men working in the aid industry or Security providers employed by aid agencies' (Mazurana & Donnelly, 2017, p. 2).

The aid worker security database concluded that:

> most of the aid workers affected by major violence were nationals of the country they were working in, whether local hires of international organisations or employees of national NGOs or Red Cross/Crescent

societies. In 2016, 245 nationals were victims of major attacks, compared to 43 internationals – a fivefold difference.

(Stoddard et al., 2017, p. 3)

Although when we take into account that the number of international staff was much lower than national staff, the ratio suggests that international staff show a higher percentage of attacks. However, if we take into account that national staff are less likely to report attacks, that they are offered less psychosocial support than international staff, and the fact that many national staff are evidencing high levels of trauma symptoms, there are clear concerns for the mental health of national staff, and the need to prioritise implementation of an equitable psychosocial support service for all staff.

My experience and that of many other aid workers is that national staff support is either non-existent or sub-par.

As far as I know there are no psychosocial care options provided for national staff. They don't get health insurance and the only psychosocial care international staff are offered is via our health insurance – and normally resources have to be found back in home countries. Some options exist for [remote] support but it isn't set up for national staff to access. It is a massive service gap. I have the option of leaving and going home after a deployment where I can find support; our national staff don't have that luxury. None of what we do could be done without national staff, we need to figure out how to support them better. With a previous organisation, a mental health counsellor was brought in to speak to staff, after a staff member was shot and killed on the compound. They held group sessions with national staff, but there was no follow up support, or options to get additional support if necessary. I spoke with the counsellor and he said that many of our national staff, several who were former child soldiers, had mental health issues that should be addressed. Nothing was done to follow up.

(Karen, UK)

The Antares Foundation and CDC survey (Antares, 2012) also found that over half of Ugandan staff participants reported five or more traumatic events in their history, with national staff reporting especially staggering histories of trauma often, but not always, associated with the humanitarian crises in their home countries. Ed Walker, who wrote *Scorched Earth* (2007) whilst working in Burundi during the civil war, shared his experiences:

I was aware, during intense periods of fighting, how my stress level rose considerably. Multiply that by 200 and I guess that would be the stress many Burundians suffered. For we were rarely the target of the violence, nor were our relatives or loved ones, and we were often living in safer areas of town. The morning after a night of particularly heavy gun and mortar fire, we would meet our staff and instantly see the stress written on their faces. It put our own tiredness into perspective. They recounted a night of fleeing, lying low in ditches, being separated from loved ones and were evidently terrified. Coming to work was a chance to escape and for a while many of them brought their families to live in our gardens as there were few places they felt safe.

(Walker, 2007, p. 33)

EMDR training was conducted in Istanbul with mental health professionals, made up of 42 per cent from Syria, 32 per cent from Iraq and 7 per cent equally from Egypt, Jordan, Libya and Palestine. Participants completed 'The Need for Trauma-based Services Questionnaire', with the results concluding that 'PTSD was the most prevalent problem reported by 80% of the Iraqi participants and 69% of the Syrian participants' (Abdul-Hamid et al., 2016, p. 1). However, participants could only meet 39 per cent of these trauma-clients' needs, due to the lack of specialist trained clinicians and resources. The mental health professionals were asked for suggestions on how to improve trauma services: 'Training and supervision of qualified staff were the most important and frequent themes, creating trauma services and psychological service for refugee camps were others, and creating trauma first aid programmes in Arabic was also mentioned' (Abdul-Hamid et al., 2016, p. 3).

In 2002, shortly after the Taliban government fell in Kabul, the [CDC] dispatched a research team to Afghanistan to study the prevalence of mental trauma among civilians there. It found that 42% of Afghans suffered from post-traumatic stress disorder and 68% exhibited signs of major depression. In other words, up to 19 million of the country's 28 million people were suffering from psychological injuries. And that was a full decade of war ago.

(Badkhen, 2012)

According to the CDC, between 30 and 70 per cent of people who have lived in warzones bear the scars of post-traumatic stress disorder and depression (Badkhen, 2012).

Conclusion

The above figures highlight the high levels of trauma experienced by local and national staff and emphasise the magnitude and significance of offering equal psychosocial support to all staff. There is a great deal of work in co-evolving culturally appropriate models of psychosocial support, and organisations need to make sure all staff can get access to these services.

I visited InterHealth's Nairobi centre, to train staff in the responding in a crisis protocol and making sure it met international requirements. During the training I referred to the word 'Ubuntu' (a Nguni word and Southern African philosophy) – 'I am, because we are'. Healing from trauma can't be done individually; we need support from trauma-informed organisations, communities, teams and families, to truly heal from trauma. Van Der Kolk, a psychiatrist renowned for his work on trauma, also refers to the word Ubuntu:

> my most profound experience with healing from collective trauma was witnessing the work of the South African Truth and Reconciliation Commission, which was based on the central and guiding principle of Ubuntu ... that denotes sharing what you have, as in 'my humanity is inextricably bound up in yours.' Ubuntu recognises that true healing is impossible without recognition of our common humanity and our common destiny.
>
> (Van Der Kolk, 2014, p. 349)

Ubuntu underlines the importance of working collaboratively and respectfully; working with local communities; encouraging community engagement; and appreciating external skills and knowledge when needed.

The local and national staff I met when working in Gaziantep stay engraved in my heart. My trip was bracketed by bombings on either side, and when I returned to the safety of my home I wrote 'Freedom' to represent the many stories I heard. When trauma is healed, growth and resilience blossom, and the strength of the human spirit shines through. Surely all humanitarian aid organisations would want to nurture growth and recovery, for all their staff?

Freedom
What's freedom if you've lost your home,
if you've been forced to separate from your family through war?
Facing the death of your mother, sister, brother, father and close friends.
Fearing that your days are numbered.

As much as time is precious, it is also restrictive.
Words of freedom become chains of torture.
A culture frozen and silenced.
This is the cost of freedom for the Syrian people.
I listened to heart wrenching personal stories,
as individuals fidget at the door desperate to be heard.
'*To hear, everyday bombs.*
To hear, everyday someone killed.
No life actually, we are breathing but no life, no opportunities, nothing.
There is fear everyday there is a chance to be arrested.
The military force themselves into our lives and our homes.
Escape from war.
The effects of this do not go easily'.
As I listened to one horrific story after another my heart broke and shattered,
a representation of these individual's lives.
Trauma was alive in the room.
I watched as individuals spoke of deep-rooted trauma,
having taken residence in their bodies,
evidenced in impulsive movements, shaking, tension and pain.
There is no such thing as trauma specialist therapy available for them,
therefore they have to live with the scars of trauma for years;
breaking down self-worth, confidence and relationships.
As individuals drew a tree (representing themselves),
we discussed resources that the tree needed to stay strong and healthy,
I realised the strength of the human spirit;
the resilience of individuals when faced with adversity.
As one individual shared his story of clinging onto the branches of a tree for his life,
as opposition rebels slaughtered hundreds of people below.
After several hours he descended into a road stained with his people's blood.
Individuals shared how they had lost ten to twenty family members.
This is not something to close our doors to or turn a blind eye.
This is a world problem; this is our problem.
Each individual could represent us in this unprecedented and uncertain time.
Reach out your hand to enable these individuals to recover and stay strong,
like the tree that sways freely in the breeze.
We all have the right to breathe the air of freedom.

8 Conclusion

The complete trauma grab bag

Survival

The nature of the human spirit is resilient and strong; we thrive for survival against all odds. 'I couldn't possibly describe [PTSD] as an illness. All my research, all my years of clinical experience, had led me to believe it was a survival tool: perhaps our ultimate survival tool' (Turnbull, 2011). Trauma impacts our mind, body and spirit; it invades our internal and external world. Critical incidents, whether man-made or natural disasters, are becoming more prevalent and assiduous, creating a climate of fear. This fear creates a societal trauma spilt, between those becoming more exclusive or inclusive towards our fellow human beings. The core principles of humanity, neutrality, impartiality and independence are more necessary than ever. To heal from trauma we need a supportive trauma-informed community. As Martin Luther King reflects, 'we are caught in an inescapable network of mutuality ... whatever affects one directly, affects all indirectly' (Ramalingham, 2013, p. xi). I strongly believe healing communities and countries suffering from trauma will lead to a more cohesive, inclusive and peaceful world.

There is the light and dark side of the coin in aid work: the exposure to trauma, and the joy of life. One image that stays with me is 'the tree of life'. An aid worker in the Ebola clinic in Sierra Leone painted an image of a large tree trunk, and as the children, who had survived Ebola, left the clinic they would paint their hands and leave their handprint, creating leaves on the tree that represent survival: 'the survival tree'! When we recover from trauma we can dance freely. As the tree that sways freely in the breeze, we all have the right to breathe the air of freedom.

Unresolved trauma leads to war

I recall a colleague saying to me, 'unresolved trauma leads to war'. As someone who has suffered PTSD I understood exactly what this statement meant. Unresolved trauma does indeed lead to war, whether the struggle becomes a battle within ourselves or with those around us. We may feel alienated, threatened, withdrawn, angry, deeply sad, panicked, unable to think clearly, exhausted, have difficulty sleeping and experience intrusive thoughts. 'If recovery and healing cannot start or are interrupted, our lives will become internal warzones, where injury after injury and trauma after trauma will occur' (Hensch, 2016, p. 304).

Trauma can activate the best and worst of humanity: 'In such war-wrecked countries, the trademark symptoms of individual war trauma, depression, anguish, and hyper-aggression, leave whole populations envenomed with sectarian and ethnic mistrust, and with the certainty that only violence can end violence' (Badkhen, 2012). On the other hand, I have seen individuals do amazing things when they recover from trauma, often becoming advocates for peace and healing.

> What would the world look like if we were able to systematically heal all the traumas? I believe that the world would be a lot less violent, because we would finally begin to interrupt the insidious inter-personal and inter-generational transmission of violence and abuse. So that world I believe would be a lot more peaceful and also a lot more prosperous.
>
> (Carriere, 2013)

Salah Ahmad founded the Jiyan Foundation for Human Rights in 2005, which provides medical and psychological services across northern Iraq's Kurdish region. It offers EMDR trauma therapy training to local mental professionals. Ahmad states:

> the potential benefits for survivors of Islamic State violence, and for the region as a whole, make the investment worthwhile. If you first help a person get peace, then he will find peace in his family, and if families are at peace, then society is at peace, and if societies are at peace, then a country is at peace.
>
> (Alfred, 2015)

Post-traumatic growth

Much has been written about 'post-traumatic growth' (Joseph, 2011), where individuals who survive trauma become stronger, more resilient and turn the negative experience into something positive to help heal others. A great example of this is the Assistance Association for Political Prisoners (AAPP) based in Yangon, Myanmar, which has trained former political prisoners in counselling to offer psychosocial support to other political prisoners (Michaels, 2014). My experience of PTSD, over 20 years ago, took me on a journey where I transitioned from working in advertising to becoming a trauma specialist therapist, trainer, speaker and writer. I wanted to use my experience to help others and prevent individuals from suffering in silence for years. Findings from the UNHRC mental health guidelines noted: 'Approximately one-third also indicated some unexpected benefits associated with stress exposure during the course of humanitarian work, including realising they are stronger than they thought, feeling closer to others, deriving more enjoyment from work, and developing stronger religious faith' (UNHRC, 2013, p. 80).

All the courageous and inspiring individuals who have shared their stories within this book to help others have recovered, over time, from their trauma experiences. I wanted to end this book with their stories of post-traumatic growth.

Peter Moore, who was held hostage by Iraqi militia for 946 days in Iraq, now gives talks within the humanitarian aid sector and military to inform individuals and organisations how to stay safe and take care of their staff. Peter ends his presentations by referring to a quote from the German philosopher, Friedrich Nietzsche: 'That which does not kill us makes us stronger.'

Tristan Clements was caught up in a violent ambush in Darfur, Sudan. After recovering he became a regional risk manager, as he wanted to guide and protect others.

> Looking back, I guess overall I went through what they now term 'Post-Traumatic Growth'.... There's no magic formula – although psychologists who study such things identify factors that are more likely to increase resilience to unhealthy stress responses. Strong social networks; a robust belief system about the world around you; strong belief in what you are doing as a humanitarian; training, especially stress-inoculation training; being in a position to respond to the crisis directly, instead of being robbed of agency. Sleep helps neurons regrow. Laughter and healthy self-care practices help. Alcohol, drugs and further risk-taking behaviour increase damage to the brain at a cellular level ... we'll never forget.... But hopefully that part of us can become, overall, something that can help us grow, and not break us down.... With deep compassion and respect to my colleagues who were not as fortunate as I – and with every desire that they be spared

the negative impact of what happened that day – I truly can look back on what happened that day and 'celebrate' it as a growth event in the trajectory of my own life and I do not consider that lightly.

After suffering from cumulative stress, Steve Ryan changed his role within the humanitarian sector to a security trainer, as he wanted to ensure aid workers went into the field prepared.

A year later I had left the organisation, returned to the UK, was in a new relationship and was working as a consultant … I was no longer a field security person and I eventually became comfortable with my reinvented self-image. I had to reassess my work commitments and how much I was willing to do. Instead of talking a good 'work/life balance' I had to hunt it down. Being outside, exercise, making time for people, smiling, being present, not pursuing a grand plan but finding great comfort in predictable stability, and understanding my own psychological make up were all critical coping mechanisms. An important aspect of this has been to be involved in the training of aid workers. Whereas I had always thought training would be boring I found a new enthusiasm because this was my way of giving back to the community that I believed in.

Christoph Hensch, who suffered PTSD after being shot in Noyve Atagi, Chechen, shared his recovery process:

I thought long and hard before accepting the challenge of leading the Mandala Foundation in Melbourne, a non-governmental organisation (NGO) dedicated to the psychosocial well-being of aid workers. My next experience was working in a human resources function with Australian Red Cross, coordinating field missions to conflict and disaster areas. Both roles were important contributions to my healing journey, and opportunities to start giving back. When I got the chance to inspire and help lead the first event of recognition for Red Cross workers that were killed in the field on 17 December 2014 at Australian Red Cross, it finally seemed that a circle had closed itself and, like the satisfaction of a deep craving, other pieces of my scattered self fell into place.

(Hensch, 2016, p. 304)

Megan Nobert, who was raped whilst on deployment in South Sudan, founded 'Report the Abuse' to provide a platform for individuals to speak out safely and openly about their experiences of sexual violence, and gain access to helpful resources. She created a short video for a sexual violence course I facilitated with ILS, to send a personal message to the participants. This ended with Megan saying, 'There is light at the other side, one day you begin to forget, one day you feel better, there is hope'.

Jon Barden, contractor for DFID, concluded his story by stating:

> My time in Afghanistan was like an apprenticeship in the aid business and experiences, both good and bad, served as a steep learning curve. The security incidents taught me about my own physical and mental limits although, with the latter, the lessons took a long time to learn. They also taught me, at the time, that one's security and mental health were one's own responsibility as no one else was going to take care of them. Fortunately times are changing and organisations are paying much more attention to these things now. As a team leader, my experiences allow me to note the signs of possible PTSD in other people and when I can say that I speak from personal experience it makes them more inclined to listen to me in an area which is historically very difficult for people to talk about.

Final thoughts

The good news is that humanitarian organisations are beginning to prioritise psychosocial support. Nomad, a travel health organisation, work with a large range of clients – from the media, to humanitarian organisations, to expedition groups:

> we have seen an increasing requirement from all industries for us to be able to provide psychosocial support whether it be pre, mid or post assignment or trauma crisis support. Employees mental wellbeing is starting to be seen at the top of the list of employers' requirements when engaging around travel health services needed for their teams.
>
> (Laura Burke, Nomad General Manager, UK)

This book has taken you on a journey of understanding trauma, highlighting the psychological risk to aid workers, explaining the physiology of trauma, sharing in-depth case studies to explore therapeutic trauma models, exploring coping strategies, managing critical incidents, highlighting pathways of care throughout deployments, and discussing the cultural relevance of trauma psychosocial services.

Aid workers have shared their personal trauma stories so as to inform organisations, and help individuals who may become impacted by acute stress or trauma. There is a great deal of discussion on psychosocial support for aid workers at global mental health conferences. It is time to turn these discussions into actions, and make sure national and local staff have access to psychosocial support, that there are clear pathways of care throughout an aid worker's deployment, and that the implementation of a robust critical incident policy and a trauma management programme are in force; psychologically preparing, strengthening and building the resilience of staff.

> The trauma field is dishonourably characterised by 'lessons learnt, lessons forgotten'. The cycle must stop. Practitioners and administrators have a responsibility to be familiar with the best evidence available to prepare strategic responses to major incidents and how to implement them effectively.
>
> (Alexander, 2015, p. 21)

We need to embed these psychosocial practices into an organisation's culture. Trauma exposure is a foreseeable risk, and there is sufficient research to confirm that the impact of trauma exposure can have a detrimental impact on an individual's mental health, including risk of burnout, acute stress and traumatic stress. The material in this book aims to provide guidance to organisations and individuals, and hopefully encourage consistent good quality psychosocial support within the humanitarian aid sector. Let's lead by example, let's be at the forefront of good psychosocial and trauma care and let's ensure that organisations and individuals are competently trauma-informed. Individuals are speaking out more about mental health struggles in order to help break through organisational stigma and challenge the 'be tough' mentality, and some senior managers are leading by example, by role-modelling good self-care and attending psychosocial support sessions. I hope that by reading this book the reader feels more stress and trauma-informed when developing skills to strengthen themselves and support their colleagues, or anyone else, if faced with challenging situations or critical incidents. It is vital to value staff's physical and psychological health and wellbeing; the carers of our world need to be cared for. As a national member of staff eloquently stated when referring to organisation's duty of care, 'we need a stable ground, and someone to take care of it'.

Sources of help

Medical and psychosocial staff care

Nomad

Offer a holistic package of care including: medical, psychological and occupational health services. Medical screenings, travel health clinics and pharmacy. Pre-, during and post-deployment resilience briefings. Trauma, burnout and stress specialist support services. Training in stress and trauma awareness, resilience building, psychological first aid and peer support programmes.

Website: www.nomadtravel.co.uk/

Thrive Worldwide

Encourage and resource people and organisations, who are creating a better world, to thrive – body, mind and spirit. We do this by providing clinical, learning and consultancy services. Our clinical services include psychological health support pre-deployment, trauma support, online counselling and confidential reviews post-mission.

Website: www.interhealthworldwide.org/

ToHealth

Offer medical, psychological and occupational health services. Head office based in Waterloo, London. Offer travel health appointments and pharmacy, and wellbeing days. Cater for all your medical and psychosocial needs.

Website: www.interhealthworldwide.org/

HealthLink 360

> *Healthlink 360 is a specialist healthcare charity with over 30 years of experience. They provide medical, psychological and travel health care to individuals and organisations. (Scotland)*
>
> Website: www.mandalastaffsupport.org/

Specialist psychosocial support

Antares Foundation

> *The Antares Foundation is a non-profit organisation based in the Netherlands. They work across all ranges and aspects of staff care and psychosocial support for humanitarian and developmental organisations worldwide.*
>
> Website: www.antaresfoundation.org

Centre for Humanitarian Psychology

> *The Centre for Humanitarian Psychology is dedicated to the professionalisation of aid workers in mental and psychosocial health in emergency contexts. (Geneva, Switzerland)*
>
> Website: www.humanitarian-psy.org

FD Consultants

> *The author of this book, Fiona Dunkley, founded FD Consultants, a network of psychotherapist and trainers offering psychosocial support and trauma specialist services. Services included pre-, mid-, and post-deployment briefings, trauma specialist and crisis response services, and training. (UK)*
>
> Website: www.fionadunkley.com

Headington Institute

> *Psychological and spiritual support for humanitarian aid workers worldwide. Strengthens humanitarian organisations by promoting the wellbeing of their staff. (California, USA)*
>
> Website: www.headington-institute.org

KonTerra Group

The KonTerra Group exists to support the health and effectiveness of organisations and their people through their process of clarity, resilience and learning. (Washington, USA)

Website: www.konterragroup.net

Mandala Staff Support

Mandala staff support is a group of psychologists providing psychosocial support, training and resources to aid workers and their organisations. (Melbourne, Australia)

Website: www.mandalastaffsupport.org

International SOS Foundation

The International SOS Foundation is dedicated to improving the health, safety and security of mobile workers around the world.

Website: www.internationalsos.com

CIC – Employment Assistance Programme (EAP)

Improve employee wellbeing and managing mental health at work.

Website: www.cic-eap.co.uk

Amani counselling centre

Helping people in developing nations by providing education and life-sustaining services to those in need. Helping those who help others.

Website: http://amanifoundation.org/about

Trauma specialist support

Trauma Aid UK – EMDR humanitarian assistance programmes

Respond to psychological trauma and distress by providing training in EMDR and traumatology to qualified mental health workers in the countries affected.

Website: www.traumaaiduk.org/

The Community Stress Prevention Center (CSPC)

Based in Israel, the CSPC deal with the treatment and prevention of psycho-trauma, promotes stress and crisis management worldwide.
Website: www.eng.icspc.org/

Tree of Life Trauma Model

Culturally sensitive models for people affected by trauma.
Website: http://dulwichcentre.com.au/the-tree-of-life/

Humanitarian networks and online information

Fifty Shades of Aid
Global Aid Worker
Humanitarian Women's Network
Humanitarian Leadership Academy
Secret Aid Worker – The Guardian

Security support

Clarity

Security training courses, support and resources.
Website: www.claritysecuritytraining.com

European Interagency Security Forum (EISF)

An independent network of Security Focal Points who represent European-based humanitarian NGOs operating internationally.
Website: www.eisf.eu

Global Journalist Security

US hostile environments trainer for journalists, non-profits and corporations. Worldwide.
Website: www.journalistsecurity.net

International Location Safety (ILS)

ILS is a security risk management consultancy that offers innovative and intelligent safety and security solutions to international organisations worldwide.
Website: www.locationsafety.com

Humanitrain

Security, health, safety, field first aid and wellbeing training.
Website: http://humanitrain.com

SOS International

Medical and travel security assistance company.
Website: www.internationalsos.com

Safer Edge

Provides practical and relevant risk management advice and instruction.
Website: www.saferedge.com/

RedR

Training, mentoring and technical support for NGOs, aid workers and communities responding to humanitarian crisis.
Website: www.redr.org.uk

Sexual violence

Report the Abuse

Breaking the silence against and within the humanitarian and development community.
Website: www.reporttheabuse.org

Inter-Agency Standing Committee (IASC)

IASC senior focal points on sexual harassment and abuse of aid workers.
Website: https://interagencystandingcommittee.org/iasc-senior-focal-points-sexual-harassment-and-abuse-aid-workers

Kidnapping and hostage-taking

Hostage UK

An independent charity that supports hostages and their families, during and after a kidnap.

Website: http://hostageuk.org

Hostage US

Hostage US is here to help you to deal with the human dynamics of a kidnapping.

Website: https://hostageus.org

Humanitarian policy guidance

CHS Alliance

Committed to improving humanitarian and development work through the application of standards.

Website: www.chsalliance.org

Duty of Care International

Provides knowledge, advice and learning for organisations globally on all aspects of Duty of Care and people management.

Website: http://dutyofcareinternational.co.uk

Humanitarian Practice Network

An independent forum for policy-makers and practitioners, working in the humanitarian sector.

Website: www.odihpn.org

Insurance

CIGNA

Health care solutions for NGOs.

Website: www.ngohealthbenefits.com

Healix International

Offers medical, security and travel assistance services.
Website: www.healix-international.com

Legal

Proelium Law

Internationally focused legal advice and support for high-risk and complex jurisdictions.
Website: https://proeliumlaw.com/

References

Abdul-Hamid, W. K. (2011) Thematic paper: the need for a category of 'religious and spiritual problems' in ICD-11. *International Psychiatry* 8: 60–61.

Abdul-Hamid, W. K. & Hughes, J. H. (2015) Integration of religion and spirituality into trauma psychotherapy: an example in Sufism? *Journal of EMDR Practice and Research* 9(3): 150–156.

Abdul-Hamid, W., Hacker Hughes, J. & Morgan, S. (2016) The need for trauma-based services in the Middle East: a pilot study. *Jacobs Journal of Psychiatry and Behavioural Science* 2(2): 1–5.

Acas (2012) Defining an employer's duty of care. Available at: www.acas.org.uk/index.aspx?articleid=3751.

ACT Alliance (2015) The World Humanitarian Summit: putting people at the centre. ACT Alliance Humanitarian Policy and Practice Advisory Group (HPPG) position paper for the World Humanitarian Summit. January. Available at: http://act alliance.org/wp-content/uploads/2015/12/J3734-ACT-Alliance-position-paper-for-World-Humanitarian-Summit_AW.pdf.

Adshed, G. & Ferris, S. (2007) Treatment of victims of trauma. *Advances in Psychiatric Treatment* 13: 358–368.

Ager, A., Pasha, E., Yu, G., Duke, T., Eriksson, C. & Cardozo, B. L. (2012) Stress, mental health, and burnout in national humanitarian aid workers in Gulu, northern Uganda. *Journal Trauma Stress* 25(6): 713–720.

Alexander, D. (2015) *Early Interventions in War and Disasters. Early Interventions for Trauma: Proceedings from Symposium held on: 25th Nov. 2014 and 8th Jan. 2015.* The British Psychological Society: Crisis, Disaster & Trauma Psychology Section.

Alfred, C. (2015) New trauma therapy may help Yazidi survivors of ISIS massacre. *Huffington Post*. Available at: www.huffingtonpost.com/entry/yazidis-movement-desensitization-and-reprocessing-therapy_us_565f76d2e4b079b 2818d2a65.

Allen, B., Brymer, M. J., Steinberg, A. M., Vernberg, E., Jacobs, A., Speier, A. & Pynoos, R. (2010) Perceptions of psychological first aid among providers responding to Hurricanes Gustav and Ike. *Journal of Traumatic Stress* 23(4): 509–513.

American Psychiatric Association (APA) (2013) *Diagnostic and Statistical Manual of Mental Disorders* (DSM-5). Arlington: American Psychiatric Association.

Antares Foundation (2012) *Managing Stress in Humanitarian Workers: Guidelines for Good Practice.* 3rd edn. Amsterdam: Antares Foundation. Available at: www.antaresfoundation.org/FileLibrary/file6782.pdf.

Arukah (2017) Available at: www.arukahnetwork.org/.

Azhar, M. H., Varma, S. L. & Dharap, A. S. (1994) Religious psychotherapy in anxiety disorder patients. *Acta Psychiatrica Scandinavica* 90(1): 1–3.

BACP (2016) *Ethical Framework for the Counselling Professions.* UK: BACP.

Badkhen, A. (2012) Afghanistan: PTSDland. Pulitzer Center. Available at: http://pulitzercenter.org/reporting/afghanistan-ptsdland.

Bayne R. & Jinks, G. (2013) *Applied Psychology: Research Training and Practice.* 2nd edn. London: SAGE.

BBC Newsnight (2016) Testimony from the South Sudan attack. 22 August. Available at: www.youtube.com/watch?v=tYoIRwm8iX8.

Bensimon, M., Amir, D. & Wolf, Y. (2008) Drumming through trauma: music therapy with post-tramatic soldiers. *The Arts in Psychotherapy* 35: 34–48.

Bremner, J. D. (2006) Traumatic stress: effects on the brain. *Dialogues in Clinical Neuroscience* 8(4): 445–461.

Bremner, J. D., Randall, P., Scott, T. M., Bronen, R. A., Seibyl, J. P., Southwick, S. M., Delaney, R. C., McCarthy, G., Charney, D. S. & Innis, R. B. (1995) MRI-based measurement of hippocampal volume in patients with combat-related stress disorder. *AM J Psychiatry* 152(7): 973–981.

Breslau, N. (1998) Epidemiology of trauma and post-traumatic stress disorder. In R. Yehunda (Ed.) *Psychological Trauma* (pp. 1–29). Washington, DC: American Psychiatric Association.

Brewin, C. R., Fuchkan, N. & Huntley, Z. (2009) Evaluation of the NHS trauma response to the London bombings. Final report to the Department of Health.

Brewin, C. R., Scragg, P., Robertson, M. & Thompson, M. (2008) Promoting mental health following the London bombings: a screen and treat approach. *Journal of Traumatic Stress* 21(1): 3–8.

Brown, K. W., Ryan, R. M. & Creswell, J. D. (2007) Mindfulness: theoretical foundations and evidence for its salutary effects. *Psychological Inquiry* 18: 211–237.

Brymer, M., Jacobs, A., Layne, C., Pynoos, R., Ruzek, J., Steinberg, A., Vernberg, E. & Watson, P. (2006) *Psychological First Aid: Field Operations Guide.* 2nd edn. Los Angeles: National Child Traumatic Stress Network and National Center for PTSD.

Cantopher, T. (2012) *Depressive Illness: The Curse of the Strong.* London: Sheldon Press.

Cardozo, B., Crawford, G., Eriksson, C., Zhu, J., Sabi, M., Ager, A., Foy, D., Snider, L., Scholte, W., Kaiser, R., Olff, M., Rijnen, B. & Simon, W. (2012) Psychological distress, depression, anxiety, and burnout among international humanitarian aid workers: a longitudinal study. *PLoS One* 7(9): e44948.

Carriere, R. (2013) Healing trauma; healing humanity. TEDx. 6 December. Available at: www.youtube.com/watch?v=CcXqcQecRXo.

Carter, C. (2015) The impact of disaster. TED Talks. TEDxBrighton. Available at: www.youtube.com/watch?v=UyTDFU0ZOPI.

Clements, T. (2010) World Humanitarian Day: the ambush (part 1). *Wanderlust, Notes from a Global Nomad.* 18 August. Available at: https://morealtitude.word-press.com/2010/08/18/world-humanitarian-day-2010-the-ambush-part-i-of-3/.

Cohen, J. A. (2006) *Treating Trauma and Traumatic Grief in Children and Adolescents.* New York: Guilford Press.

Connorton, E., Perry, M., Hemenway, D. & Miller, M. (2011) Humanitarian relief workers and trauma-related mental illness. *Epidemiologic Reviews* 34(1): 145–155.

Core Humanitarian Standard (CHS) (2015) CHS guidance notes and indicators. In alliance with CHS, the Sphere Project & Groupe URD. Available at: https://corehumanitarianstandard.org/files/files/CHS-Guidance-Notes-and-Indicators.pdf.

Craig, G. (2011) *EFT Emotional Freedom Technique: The EFT Manual.* California: Energy Psychology Press.

Davidson, S. (2010) The development of the British Red Cross' psychosocial framework 'CALMER'. *Journal of Social Work Practice* 24(1): 29–42.

Deahl, M., Srinivasan, M., Jones, N., Neblett, C. & Jolly, A. (2001) Evaluating psychological debriefings: are we measuring the right outcomes? *Journal of Traumatic Stress* 14: 157–529.

Dein, S. (2006) Religion, spirituality and depression: implications for research and treatment. *Primary Care and Community Psychiatry* 11(2): 67–72.

Denborough, D. (2008) *Collective Narrative Practice: Responding to Individuals, Groups, and Communities Who Have Experienced Trauma.* Adelaide: Dulwich Centre Publications.

Dobson, K. S. & Block, L. (1988) Historical and philosophical bases of cognitive behavioural theories. *Handbook of Cognitive Behavioural Therapies.* London: Guilford Press.

Donnelly, L. (2017) Don't offer counseling to terror survivors: it could make trauma worse, says Britain's top psychiatrist. *Telegraph.* 12 June. Available at: www.telegraph.co.uk/news/2017/06/12/dont-offer-counselling-terror-survivors-could-make-trauma/.

Dryregrov, A. (1989) Caring for helpers in disaster situations: psychological debriefing. *Disaster Management* 2: 25–30.

Dryregrov, A. & Regel, S. (2012) Early interventions following exposure to traumatic events: implications for practice from recent research. *Journal of Loss and Trauma* 17: 271–291.

Dunkley, F. (2017) 12 years of trauma: from the 7/7 bombings (2005) to the Grenfell Tower fire (2017). *Counselling at Work* 95: 16–20.

Dunkley, F. & Claridge, M. (2012) Eye movement desensitisation and reprocessing (EMDR) in practice at Transport for London. *Counselling at Work* 72: 4–9.

Ehlers, A., Clark, D. M., Hackman, A., McManus, F. & Fennell, M. (2005) Cognitive therapy for post-traumatic stress disorder: development and evaluation. *Behaviour, Research and Therapy* 43(4): 413–431.

Ehlers, A., Grey, N., Wild, J., Stott, R., Liness, S., Deale, A., Handley, R., Albert, I., Cullen, D., Hackmann, A., Manley, J., McManus, F., Brady, F., Salkovkis, P. & Clark, D. (2013) Implementation of cognitive therapy for PTSD in routine clinical care: effectiveness and moderators of outcome in a consecutive sample. *Behaviour Research and Therapy* 51(11): 742–752.

Englund, H. (1998) Death, trauma and ritual: Mozambican refugees in Malawi. *Social Science & Medicine* 46(9): 1165–1174.

Eriksson, C. B., Kemp, H. V., Gorsuch, R., Hoke, S. & Foy, D. W. (2012) Trauma exposure and PTSD symptoms in international relief and development personnel. *Journal of Traumatic Stress* 14(1): 205–212.

Fast, L. (2014) *Aid in Danger: The Perils and Promise of Humanitarianism*. Philadelphia: University of Pennsylvania Press.

Gatchel, R. J. & Rollings, K. H. (2008) Evidence-informed management of chronic low back pain with cognitive behavioural therapy. *The Spine Journal* 8(1): 40–44.

Graham, M. C. (2014) *Facts of Life: Ten Issues of Contentment*. Colorado: Outskirts Press.

Greenberg, N., Langston, V. & Jones, N. (2008) Trauma Risk Management (TRiM) in the UK armed forces. *Journal of the Royal Army Medical Corps* 154: 124–127.

Greenwood, G. & Harmes, L. (2017) Fire staff on long-term mental health leave up by 30%. BBC News. 17 September. Available at: www.bbc.co.uk/news/uk-41164996.

Hamblen, J. & Slone, L. (2016) *Research Findings on the Traumatic Stress Effects of Terrorism*. National Center for PTSD. U.S. Department of Veterans Affairs. Available at: www.ptsd.va.gov/professional/trauma/disaster-terrorism/research-findings-traumatic-stress-terrorism.asp.

Harris, D. A. (2007) Dance/movement therapy approaches to fostering resilience and recovery among African adolescent torture survivors. *Torture* 17(2): 134–155.

Hawker, D. (2016) *Debriefing Aid Workers and Missionaries: A Comprehensive Manual*. 12th edn. London: CHSAlliance.

Hawker, D. M., Durkin, J. & Hawker, D. S. J. (2011) To debrief or not to debrief our heroes: that is the question. *Clinical Psychology and Psychotherapy* 18: 453–463.

Hebb, D. O. (1949) *The Organisation of Behaviour*. New York: Wiley & Sons.

Hensch, C. (2016) Twenty years after Novye Atagi: a call to care for the carers. *International Review of the Red Cross* 98(1): 299–314.

Herman, J. (1997) *Trauma and Recovery: The Aftermath of Violence – from Domestic Abuse to Political Terror*. New York: Perseus Books Group.

Hess, D. (2017) Duty of care goes local. The Konterra Group. Available at: www.konterragroup.net/duty-care-goes-local/.

Hobfoll, S., Watson, P., Bell, C., Brymer, M., Friedman, M. J., Friedman, M., Gersons, B., de Jong, J., Layne, C., Maguen, S., Neria, Y., Norwood, A., Pynoos, R., Reissman, D., Ruzek, J., Shalev, A., Soloman, Z., Steinberg, A. & Ursano, R. (2007) Five essential elements of immediate and mid-term mass trauma intervention: empirical evidence. *Psychiatry* 70(4): 283–315.

Huddlestone, L. M., Paton, D. & Stephens, C. (2006) Conceptualising traumatic stress in police officers: pre-employment, critical incidents and organisational influences. *Traumatology* 12: 170–177.

Inter-Agency Standing Committee (IASC) (2007) *IASC Guidelines on Mental Health and Psychosocial Support in Emergency Settings.* Geneva: IASC.

Inter-Agency Standing Committee (IASC) (2017) *A Common Monitoring and Evaluation Framework for Mental Health and Psychosocial Support in Emergency Settings.* Geneva: IASC.

International Medical Corps (IMC) (2017) Mental health. Available at: www.internationalmedicalcorps.org.uk/saving-lives/all-survival/mental-health.

International Red Cross and Red Crescent Movement (1965) *The 20th International Conference of the Red Cross and Red Crescent; United Nations (UN) General Assembly Resolution 46/182, 19 December 1991; and UN General Assembly Resolution 58/114, 5 February 2004.*

Iribarren, J., Prolo, P., Neagos, N. & Chiappelli, F. (2005) Post-traumatic stress disorder: evidence-based research for the third millennium. *Evidence-Based Complementary and Alternative Medicine* 2(4): 503–512.

Jeanette, J. M. & Scoboria, A. (2008) Firefighter preferences regarding post-incident intervention. *Work & Stress* 22: 314–326.

Jones, A. (2015) Sexual assault blog. 18 November. Headington Institute. Available at: http://headington-institute.org/blog-home/511/sexual-assault.

Jones, E., Denman, K. & Molloy, E. (2017) Managing the security of aid workers with diverse profiles. Paper presented to the European Interagency Security Forum (EISF<HS>) Annual Forum, XL Catlin London, 5 October.

Joseph, S. (2011) *What Doesn't Kill Us: The New Psychology of Post-Traumatic Growth.* New York: Perseus Books Group.

Kabat-Zinn, J. (2005) *Wherever You Go There You Are: Mindfulness Meditation in Everyday Life.* New York: Hyperion.

Kinchin, D. (2001) *Post Traumatic Stress Disorder: The Invisible Injury.* Oxfordshire: Success Unlimited.

Leach, A. (2015) Exporting trauma: can the talking cure do more harm than good? *Guardian.* 5 February.

Levine, J. (1997) *Waking the Tiger: Healing Trauma.* California: North Atlantic Book.

Lucey, A. (2017) Meaning lost and found: containment in contemporary organisations. A case study based research project with a crisis agency. Unpublished doctoral thesis.

MacLean, P. (1990) *The Triune Brain in Evolution: Role in Paleocerebral Functions.* New York: Springer.

Management of Health and Safety at Work (1999) Available at: www.legislation.gov.uk/uksi/1999/3242/pdfs/uksi_19993242_en.pdf.

Manji, H., Drevets, W. & Chaney, D. (2001) The cellular neurobiology of depression. *Nature Medicine* 7(5): 541–547.

Manzoni, G. M., Pagnini, F., Castelnuovo, G. & Molinari, E. (2008) Relaxation training for anxiety: a ten-years systematic review with meta-analysis. *BMC Psychiatry*: 8–41.

Maxfield, L. (2014) Commemorating EMDR's 25th anniversary by highlighting EMDR humanitarian projects. *Journal of EMDR Practice and Research* 8(4): 179–180.

Mazurana, D. & Donnelly, P. (2017) Stop the sexual assault against humanitarian and development aid workers. Feinstein International Center. Available at: http://fic.tufts.edu/assets/Sexual-Assault-Aid-Workers-research-brief-Dec-2016-FIC.pdf.

Michaels, S. (2014) Burma's former political prisoners offer counselling for trauma. *The Irrawaddy*. February.

Mitchell, J. T. (1983) When disaster strikes ... the critical incident debriefing process. *Journal of the Emergency Medical Services* 8: 36–39.

Mitchell, J. T. & Everly, G. S. (1997) The scientific evidence for critical incident stress management. *Journal of Emergency Medical Services* 22: 86–93.

Napier, N. (1996) *Recreating Your Self: Increasing Self-Esteem through Imaging and Self-Hypnosis*. New York: W. W. Norton & Company.

Newberg, A. & Waldman, M. R. (2009) *How God Changes Your Brain: Breakthrough Findings from a Leading Neuroscientist*. New York: Ballantine Books.

NICE (2005) *Post-Traumatic Stress Disorder (PTSD): The Management of PTSD in Adults and Children in Primary and Secondary Care (Full Clinical Guideline 26 Developed by the National Collaborating Centre for Mental Health)*. London: National Institute for Health and Clinical Excellence. Available at: www.nice.org.uk/guidance/cg26/evidence/full-guideline-including-appendices-113-pdf-193442221.

Nobert, M. (2017) *Humanitarian Experiences with Sexual Violence: Compilation of Two Years of Report the Abuse Data Collection*. Report the Abuse. Available at: https://interagencystandingcommittee.org/system/files/rta_humanitarian_experiences_with_sexual_violence_-_compilation_of_two_years_of_report_the_abuse_data_collection.pdf.

Nowlan, K. (2014) Trauma support: let's prepare not scare. *Counselling at Work* 9–13.

O'Donnell, K. (2017) Unbreakable? Recognising humanitarian stress and trauma. MHN, a global community of mental health innovators. 17 October. Available at: www.mhinnovation.net/blog/2017/oct/17/unbreakable-recognizing-humanitarian-stress-and-trauma.

Ogden, P. & Fisher, J. (2015) *Sensorimotor Psychotherapy: Interventions for Trauma and Attachment*. New York: W. W. Norton & Company.

Pardess, E. (2005) Training and mobilizing volunteers for emergency response and long-term support. *Journal of Aggression, Maltreatment and Trauma* 10(1–2): 609–620.

Parnell, L. (2007) *A Therapist's Guide to EMDR: Tools and Techniques for Successful Treatment*. New York: W. W. Norton & Company.

People in Aid & InterHealth (2009) *Approaches to Staff Care in International NGOs*. UK: InterHealth & People in Aid.

Peters, S. (2012) *The Chimp Paradox: The Mind Management Programme for Confidence, Success and Happiness*. Croydon: Ebury Publishing.

Porges, S. (2001) The polyvagal theory: phylogenetic substrates of a social network system. *International Journal of Psychophysiology* 42: 123–146.

Ramalingham, B. (2013) *Aid on the Edge of Chaos*. Oxford: Oxford University Press.

Raphael, B. (1986) *When Disaster Strikes: How Individuals and Communities Cope with Catastrophe*. New York: Basic Books.

Razali, S. M., Hasanah, C. I., Aminah, K. & Subramaniam, M. (1998) Religious-sociocultural psychotherapy in patients with anxiety and depression. *Australian and New Zealand Journal of Psychiatry* 32(6): 867–872.

Rebb, J. & Atkins, P. W. B. (2015) *Mindfulness in Organisations*. Cambridge: Cambridge University Press.

Robinson, R. C., Mitchell, J. T. & Murdock, P. (1995) The debate on psychological debriefings. *Australian Journal of Emergency Care* 2: 6–7.

Rose, S., Bisson, J., Churchill, R. & Wessely, S. (2009) Psychological debriefing for preventing post traumatic stress disorder (PTSD). Cochrane Database of Systematic Reviews. Available at: www.ncbi.nlm.nih.gov/pubmed/12076399.

Rothschild, B. (2000) *The Body Remembers: The Psychotherapy of Trauma and Trauma Treatment*. New York and London: W. W. Norton & Company.

Rothschild, B. (2017) *The Body Remembers Volume 2: Revolutionizing Trauma Treatment*. New York and London: W. W. Norton & Company.

Rowe, A. (2010) Whatever gets you through today: an examination of cynical humour among emergency service professionals. *Journal of Loss and Trauma* 15(5): 448–464.

Rudge, P. & Regel, S. (2014) Taken hostage. *Counselling at Work* 9–13.

Sack, M., Hopper, J. W. & Lamprecht, F. (2004) Low respiratory sinus arrhythmia and prolonged psychophysiological arousal in posttraumatic stress disorder: heart rate dynamics and individual differences in arousal regulation. *Biological Psychiatry* 55(3): 284–290.

Saul, J. (2014) *Collective Trauma, Collective Healing*. New York: Routledge.

Schauer, M., Neuner, F. & Elbert, T. (2005) *Narrative Exposure Therapy: A Short-Term Intervention for Traumatic Stress Disorders after War, Terror, or Torture*. Cambridge: Hogrefe & Huber Publishers.

Schreter, L. & Harmer, A. (2013) Delivering aid in highly insecure environments: A critical review of the literature, 2007–2012. London: DFID. Available at: https://assets.publishing.service.gov.uk/media/57a08a4c40f0b64974000522/60995-Delivering_aid_in_highly_insecure_environments_final_report.pdf.

Schuppener, C. & Schuppener, J. (2016) *Back Home: Living with Change After Time Abroad*. Norderstedt: Books on Demand.

Shapiro, E. (2009) EMDR treatment of recent trauma. *Journal of EMDR Practice and Research* 3(3): 141–151.

Shapiro, F. (1989) Efficacy of the eye movement desensitization procedure in the treatment of traumatic memories. *Journal of Traumatic Stress* 2: 199–223.

Shapiro, F. (2001) *Eye Movement Desensitization and Reprocessing: Basic Principles, Protocols and Procedures*. 2nd edn. New York: Guilford Press.

Shapiro, F. (2004) *EMDR: The Breakthrough 'Eye Movement' Therapy for Overcoming Anxiety, Stress and Trauma*. New York: Basic Books.

Shapiro, F. (2005) *EMDR Solutions: Pathways to Healing*. New York: W. W. Norton & Company.

Shapiro, F. (2006) *EMDR: Case Formulation, Principles, Forms, Scripts and Worksheets*. UK: EMDR Institute.

Shifting the Power project (2016) *Shifting the Power: Year 02 2016 Overview.* Start Network & UK Aid.

Siegel, D. J. (2010) *Mindsight: The New Science of Personal Transformation.* New York: Bantam Books.

The Sphere Guidebook (2011) *Humanitarian Charter and Minimum Standards in Humanitarian Response.* The Sphere Project.

Sphere Project (2004) *Humanitarian Charter and Minimum Standards in Disaster Response.* Geneva: Sphere Project.

Stoddard, A., Harmer, A. & Czwarno, M. (2017) *Aid Worker Security Report 2017. Behind the Attacks: A Look at the Perpetrators of Violence against Aid Workers.* Aid Workers Security Data. Humanitarian Outcomes.

Stoddard, A., Harmer, A. & DiDomenico, V. (2009) *Providing Aid in Insecure Environments: 2009 Update* (The Humanitarian Policy Brief 34). New York: Center for International Cooperation at New York University.

Stuber, J., Galea, S., Boscarino, J. A. & Schlesinger, M. (2006) Was there unmet mental health need after the September 11, 2001 terrorist attacks? *Social Psychiatry and Psychiatric Epidemiology* 41(3): 230–240.

Tehrani, N. (2010) Compassion fatigue: experiences in occupational health, human resources, counselling and police. *Occupational Medicine* 60(2): 133–138.

Tuckey, M. & Scott, J (2014) Group critical incident stress debriefing with emergency services personnel: a randomized controlled trial. *Anxiety Stress Coping* 27(1): 38–54.

Turnbull, G. (2011) *Trauma, from Lockerbie to 7/7: How Trauma Affects Our Minds and How We Fight Back.* London: Bantam Press.

Turner, S. W., Thompson, J. & Rosser, R. M. (1995) The Kings Cross fire: psychological reactions. *Journal of Traumatic Stress* 8(3): 419–427.

UNHRC (2013) Mental health and psychosocial support for staff. July. Available at: www.unhcr.org/51f67bdc9.pdf.

Van Der Kolk, B. (2014) *The Body Keeps the Score: Mind, Brain and Body in the Transformation of Trauma.* London: Penguin Books.

Van Der Kolk, B., Stone, L., West, J., Rhodes, A., Emerson, D., Suvak, M. & Spinazzola, J. (2014) Yoga as an adjunctive treatment for PTSD. *Journal of Clinical Psychiatry* 75(6): 559–565.

Walker, E. (2007) *Reflections from the Scorched Earth: A Witness from Some of the World's Toughest War Zones.* Oxford: Monarch Books.

Wall, I. (2015) Gloves off between local and international NGOs. Available at: www.irinnews.org/analysis/2015/10/22.

Weiss, D. S. (2007) The impact of event scale-revised. In J. P. Wilson & T. M. Keane (Eds) *Assessing Psychological Trauma and PTSD: A Practitioner's Handbook.* 2nd edn (pp. 168–189). New York: Guilford Press.

Welton-Mitchell, C. E. (2013) UNHCR's mental health and psychosocial support: for staff. July. Geneva: United Nations High Commissioner for Refugees Policy Development & Evaluation Service.

Wilson, P. & Long, I. (2009) *The Big Book of Blob Trees.* Oxon: Speechmark Publishing Ltd.

World Health Organization (2008) *IASC Guidelines on Mental Health and Psychosocial Support in Emergency Settings: Checklist for Field Use*. Geneva: Inter-Agency Standing Committee.

World Health Organization, War Trauma Foundation & World Vision International (2011) *Psychological First Aid: Guide for Field Workers*. Geneva: WHO.

Index

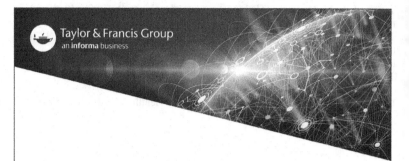

Printed in the United States
by Baker & Taylor Publisher Services